D1765769

Teaching With AI

Empowering Educators for the Future Classroom—
Unlock Learning Potential, Save Time, and Simplify
the Complexities of Integration in Education

ModernMind Publications

Contents

Introduction

To understand the future of technology, we need to begin with one fundamental truth: Technology is natural. –Gray Scott

As educators, we face challenging decisions every day as we try to navigate the complexities of today's classrooms. Classrooms packed with students, individuals with varying levels of knowledge, and the never-ending mission to inspire and prepare the future generation—all put our expertise to the test and push us to think beyond the box.

Gray Scott's words are especially thought-provoking when considering whether or not we should incorporate AI in education. It demonstrates that the out-of-the-box philosophy of artificial intelligence in the classroom is the next logical step in the evolution of teaching and learning. In the same way that people have always tried to understand and fit into their surroundings, AI is the newest form of this desire, a tool that can help us learn and teach better.

In education, AI can tailor lessons to each student, change those lessons based on their learning capacities, and give teachers new ideas, all of which are similar to how adaption and evolution work in nature. The challenge is to employ AI responsibly and ethically, making sure technology serves a broader educational mission and doesn't replace human educators. In the end, this saying serves as a reminder that AI, like every other technology, is the result of human creativity and curiosity and that its function in education should be in sync with the human will to learn and develop.

Two Sides to Every Story

Let's consider two teachers in a nearby school, Ms. Anderson and Mr. Smith. Both love what they do and are equally passionate about achieving excellent outcomes for their students.

Ms. Anderson is a teacher with many years of experience. She is dedicated to traditional teaching methods, swearing by her chalkboard and the same lesson plans year after year. It's crucial to her that she gets to know each of her students so she can help each of them be successful. She spends hours reading assignments and giving personalized feedback in writing.

Mr. Smith, a tech-savvy educator, teaches in the classroom next door. He feels entirely in charge of his class and leverages AI to customize his lessons, change how he teaches, and give each individual the tools they need to do well.

For Mr. Smith, it's not just about using technology to make his life easier; it's also about getting more meaningful time to spend with his students. Since taxing responsibilities like grading papers can now be completed by AI, he has more time to focus on encouraging student participation. He has a work-life balance that keeps him energized in his career and focused on the things in his personal life that matter most. His students look forward to his classes because of the engaging, AI-enhanced opportunities for learning he provides in each one.

You may have already noticed some of these changes in your own experiences. Still, the striking contrast between Ms. Anderson and Mr.

Smith highlights the seismic shifts currently taking place in the educational system.

With that in mind, we've seen over and over again how hard it is to adapt to a world that is constantly changing. You may be thinking about how best to use AI's power in your classroom now that it is evolving so quickly. The worry of being outclassed by newer technologies is always on your mind. Sometimes, you might have even wondered if this technology actually helps you teach effectively or if it's just a fad that will pass in a year or two.

What made you think of picking up this book, then? Have you been naturally curious about how you can use AI since ChatGPT burst onto the scene? Was it a chat with a coworker who told you an exciting AI success story that made you want to start, but you didn't know where to begin? As each teacher is unique, so is their curiosity about AI. I'm here to talk about AI in detail, try to answer your questions, and get you moving down the path of integrating AI into your teaching.

AAA Method: Unlocking Evolution

This book is designed for dedicated professionals like you who want to use AI to its fullest in their training. This book attempts to reduce the ambiguities surrounding AI in education by providing valuable tips to make you feel more comfortable using these fantastic tools.

The AAA Method, a structured technique that includes adaptation, automation, and amplification, is the backbone of this plan. It gives you a complete framework for using AI in your teaching that reduces the complexity and overwhelm that naturally comes with learning something new. This method will teach you how to change your lessons, automate office work, and make a more significant difference as a teacher.

The time you spend reading this book will pay off in spades. You'll find helpful tips, tools, and shortcuts in each chapter that will make your professional life better in noticeable ways:

1. **Adapt:** Make your teaching program more flexible so that it can meet the needs of each student. This will increase engagement and improve results.
2. **Automate:** By automating routine administrative activities, you'll have more time for direct student instruction and mentorship.
3. **Amplify:** Find new ways to improve your teaching skills, which will increase your influence and leave a lasting impression on your students.

The final product of this experience is a colorful portrait of a brighter future as a teacher. Imagine being even more sure of yourself in the classroom, effortlessly meeting the needs of each individual. The administrative tasks are done quickly and well, and your lessons hit home with your students. Your job satisfaction is high, and your pupils love their time in your class.

Significant amounts of research, studying, and time went into compiling the information in this book. It can be challenging for educators like you to get up to speed with AI. This book will give you real-world advice.

Consider the problems you had to solve before getting the information in this book. Think about how many hours you've spent doing the same things over and over, how frustrating it is to have to teach lessons in a way that doesn't work for everyone, and how hard it is to meet all of your students' needs. This book will light the path to a better, more productive, and satisfying future.

Welcome to the beginning of a transformative journey that will redefine how you teach. By the time you're done reading this, you'll be well-equipped to incorporate AI into your classroom in ways you never thought of and maybe never thought possible. You're starting a new phase in your profession, one where your potential has never been greater.

Chapter 1

Making Sense of AI: Unlocking the Door for Evolution

Pop culture has spun wild stories about AI, portraying it in ways that were once viewed as bizarre and straight out of a science fiction movie. Similar to the adversaries in films like *The Terminator* and *The Matrix,* where AI is portrayed as a hostile entity seeking to dominate the globe, these stories imagine a world where malicious AI rises to power, conquers the planet, and gives orders.

These days, AI is much more grounded in truth. AI hasn't become our computer masters; it has become a useful part of our lives. Siri and Alexa are like our AI sidekicks, always ready to assist us by locating items, organizing our schedules, and streamlining our daily routines. Such AI systems are "narrow AI," which means they're great at certain jobs like translating languages or recognizing images, but not as smart as the super-smart computers we see in movies.

AI today is all about making things easier for people. For doctors and other medical professionals, it's like having a personal physician right at their fingertips. It's a numbers expert for finance people as it makes looking at data much easier. It even started producing original works of art and music, which is quite cool.

Furthermore, the ethical use of AI is increasing in importance every day. Laws and regulations have recently been implemented in the United States to protect people's rights and promote safety around the development and use of AI. We're talking about things like data privacy, transparency, and all that good stuff. Don't worry—AI isn't trying to take over humanity or our minds. Instead, people are using it to make their lives better.

What Exactly is AI?

When you hear the word "Artificial Intelligence," or AI for short, you may immediately think of things like ChatGPT, robots, self-driving cars, or other AI chatbots and artificially generated visuals. A deeper understanding of AI's inner workings and its consequences for the present and the future must be sought, however, and this requires looking beyond the technology's outputs.

In the 1950s, the term "AI" was first used to describe technology and tools capable of doing things that only humans had been able to do (Burns, 2022). This definition, on the other hand, is very broad and has changed over decades of constant study and technological progress.

When discussing the possibility of imbuing a computer or other machine with intelligence, it is crucial to define exactly what is meant by the term "intelligence." As it turns out, this word is what makes people unique among living things and is at the heart of the human experience. Some experts say that intelligence is the capacity to change, plan, innovate in new situations, overcome challenges, and learn new things.

Because intelligence is often seen as the core of what it means to be human, it's not strange that scientists have tried to replicate it. Some human intelligence traits may be exhibited by modern AI systems, such as the ability to learn, solve problems, perceive, and even show some creativity and social awareness.

AI is no longer something from the realm of science fiction; it is already a practical reality. Let's have a look at some common AI technologies and get an idea of how they function.

Virtual Assistants

You may be familiar with Alexa, Amazon's voice AI, or Google Assistant. Voice requests activate these AI-powered "virtual assistants." They can get information, listen to music, and operate smart home gadgets. Using natural language processing (NLP) and machine learning (ML) algorithms, they can determine what you are saying and answer appropriately.

Chatbots

Many companies and websites use tools that leverage AI to answer customer questions. Together, natural language processing and machine learning enable these chatbots to understand users' questions and supply accurate answers in real-time, every time.

Recommendation Systems

Consider the tailored suggestions you get on streaming services like Netflix and e-commerce sites like Amazon. Your past preferences and selections are analyzed by AI recommendation systems, which then use deep learning and collaborative filtering to offer content that best suits your preferences.

Autonomous Vehicles

Autonomous vehicles depend on AI to learn how to drive and make decisions in real-time, using cameras, sensors, and machine learning. This innovative technology relies on intricate algorithms for sensing, deliberation, and command.

Identifying Fraud

AI is quietly keeping your banking transactions safe. Pattern-recognizing algorithms use your buying habits to find out-of-the-ordinary activities and stop fraudulent transactions, keeping your accounts safe.

Language Translation

When you use Google Translate or other similar tools, you're using AI to translate languages. The use of AI models has greatly improved the rate and precision with which texts may be translated across languages.

Medical Diagnostics

When it comes to medical treatment, AI has made tremendous inroads. AI algorithms help radiologists figure out what medical images mean, which speeds up and improves the accuracy of diagnoses. Disease outbreak forecasting and medicine development are two such areas where AI has been put to use.

Smart Home Automation

Systems that are run by AI can help you save energy, handle your lights, and make your home safer. Heating and cooling systems can be programmed to your exact specifications with the help of devices like the Nest Thermostat.

Generating Content

These days, it's not uncommon to find news stories or product descriptions generated by AI. You might not realize it, but AI could have written the content you read (a human *did* write this book, just in case you're wondering).

These examples of AI in the real world will help you clearly understand what AI is and how it works. With this understanding under your belt, you'll be in a better position to spot AI wherever it appears and fully value its contribution to the modern world.

How Do I Use AI?

AI comes in many different forms and is in the technology we're already using every day. You can see AI in action in the smart speakers you have in your living room that connect to digital assistants like Alexa and Google. There are also well-known AI apps like ChatGPT, Google Bard, and the newly released Bing Chat.

Machine learning algorithms are behind the scenes whenever you ask Alexa for the weather or ask ChatGPT for a country's capital. Although these systems cannot replace human intelligence or social interaction, they do have the astonishing ability to learn and improve upon behaviors that were not included in their original programming.

You can use AI in almost every part of your life, and chances are good that you probably already are!

Analyzing Aspects of AI from Different Angles

There are many subfields within the field of AI, but they may be broken down into three broad categories: narrow AI, general AI, and super AI.

Narrow AI—The Expert

Artificial Narrow Intelligence (ANI), also called "narrow AI," is a key part of how voice agents like Alexa, Siri, and Google Assistant work. Intelligent systems that have been designed or taught for a narrow purpose, such as completing a specific task or solving a particular problem, but that have not been built to perform other tasks fall into this category.

While ANI may not have a human level of general intelligence, it does pretty well in specific domains. Some examples of narrow AI are speech assistants, recognition of images, tools for answering common customer service questions, and approaches for content moderation. ChatGPT is a state-of-the-art example of ANI because it was explicitly designed to generate text responses in response to user input.

General AI—The Thinker

The concept of Artificial General Intelligence (AGI), sometimes known as "strong AI," which would see robots capable of understanding and carrying out a wide variety of activities based on collected experience, remains mostly theoretical. Reasoning, abstract thought, experiential learning, and the ability to apply knowledge to new problems are all hallmarks of artificial general intelligence, which places it on par with human intelligence.

To date, no AI has achieved the degree of competency sought by AGI proponents, which includes the ability to reason abstractly, solve complex problems, and make sense of the world around it. AI researchers are working hard to create a system that is truly aware.

Super AI—The King of Change

Though still a theory, the idea of Artificial Superintelligence (ASI) is amazing and could change the course of human history. If you're getting a sci-fi vibe from it, that's because it is to some extent. AI Superintelligence is a hypothetical future when machines are so intelligent that they outperform humans in every conceivable way.

The goal of ASI is to create a system that can learn and improve on its own. Although ASI exists only in theory, if applied ethically and responsibly, it might lead to revolutionary improvements in domains like medicine and technology. The enormous potential of ASI, however, also begs the question of how responsibly it should be used and what effect it will have on society.

Machine Learning: A Breakdown

AI is distinguished from other areas of computer science by the central role played by machine learning. Machine learning, which allows computers to learn from a variety of examples rather than just those given to them, is a key component of AI that contributes to its unique ability to automate jobs without requiring any human intervention. Remember that machine learning is just one branch of artificial intelligence.

Simply put, machine learning is the process of using large datasets to strategically teach a system. This training allows the system to correct its own mistakes and recognize complex patterns, allowing it to make accurate predictions and choices in situations for which it was not specifically built.

The real-world uses of machine learning are diverse. Image and voice recognition and protecting financial transactions from fraud are just a few examples among many. Consider Facebook's built-in image recognition feature as an example. When users share a photo, the platform uses machine learning to quickly evaluate it, detect faces, and provide tags for users' different friends. The system gets better over time with constant improvement, making suggestions that are more and more correct.

The field of machine learning, which is a key part of AI, is often broken down into two broad classes: supervised and unsupervised learning.

Supervised Learning

Most AIs are taught using supervised learning, which relies on a large dataset of examples that have been labeled and organized by human specialists. A lot of data is fed into these machine learning systems, and each dataset is carefully marked up to highlight important traits. This is basically teaching by showing.

In order to teach a machine learning model something specific—say, how to tell the difference between photos of circles and squares—it must first be given a large dataset that includes examples of both shapes in a variety of settings. Each shape is carefully labeled in these photos. Then, the algorithm uses this labeled information to figure out the shapes and what makes them unique, like the fact that circles don't have corners and squares have four equal sides. The system gets very good at looking at new pictures and correctly figuring out what shapes they are made of after a lot of practice on this set of pictures.

Unsupervised Learning

When it comes to unsupervised learning, algorithms instead attempt to recognize patterns in data, looking for similarities that can be used to classify information. As an example, we can group cars with the same engine size together or stack baskets of identical fruits.

When you use unsupervised algorithms instead of supervised learning, you don't have to focus on predefined groups. Instead, they painstakingly comb through data in search of correlations and patterns that may be used for things like targeting certain groups of customers based on their preferences and buying habits.

Reinforcement Learning

When given data, a reinforcement learning system will try different strategies until it finds one that maximizes rewards. Consider teaching a computer to win in a video game by providing it with positive reinforcement when it achieves its goals and negative reinforcement when it fails to do so.

Based on the feedback it receives, the system gradually improves its ability to assess the gaming world, plan its next move strategically, and adapt to new challenges. After some training, it can play games without help and even rack up high scores. The benefits of reinforcement learning may be seen in real-world applications, where it is used to teach autonomous robots how to behave optimally in challenging settings.

Neural Networks: What are They?

Neural networks are an essential component of machine learning. The complex links between neurons in the brain are used as inspiration for these mathematical models, which try to copy how neurons talk to each other.

Let's examine this idea by drawing on the analogy of a group of robots working together to tackle a complex issue. Each robot has been tailored to identify individual pieces based on the patterns or colors they spot. These robots, as they cooperate, can pool their varied skills for a more effective strike on the puzzle. This team of robots represents a neural network in its most basic form.

Neural networks can fine-tune their internal settings, which lets them change the results they produce. A lot of data is fed into each neural network during training. This experience helps the network understand what to do when it is given certain data during the learning process.

These systems enable data transfer between nodes, thanks to many algorithmic layers that are interconnected. This structure allows us to teach neural networks to do specific tasks by changing how important input is as it moves through the layers. During training, the weights that are applied to data as it moves between layers are constantly being improved. Repeating this complex dance of tweaks, the network's output is fine-tuned until it closely matches the target value. To put it another way, the network has 'learned' how to carry out the required operation.

The Concept of Deep Learning

When it comes to AI, deep learning, which is a popular type of machine learning, is a giant leap ahead. Deep learning is all about training artificial neural networks that have three or more layers and may be used as building blocks for various tasks.

A key difference between deep-learning architectures and more conventional machine-learning models is the sheer number of layers present in deep-learning networks. One of the main things that make these networks so powerful is that they can connect hundreds of computers.

When it comes to training, deep learning isn't picky; it's happy to use either supervised or unsupervised methods, and it commonly combines the two. Because they are flexible, deep-learning models can learn in a way that is similar to how humans think.

A Flood of Applications

If all that talk about neural networks and deep learning has your head spinning, don't worry. You don't need to understand all of their intricacies to understand how they lead to real-world value.

The power of deep-learning systems to recognize subtle patterns in data is a major selling point for this type of software, which has wide application potential. To figure out how complicated human language is, Natural Language Processing uses deep learning a lot. Deep learning models help with many tasks, like translating languages, figuring out how people feel, and creating texts because they can understand the details of spoken and written language.

Another amazing use is speech recognition, which uses deep learning to comprehend the complexities of human speech. This lets voice-activated systems, like virtual assistants, correctly understand and carry out human voice commands.

Even image identification is revolutionized by deep learning. With this technology, machines can now understand the visual world and identify objects, forms, and patterns in photos with pinpoint accuracy. The technology has a wide range of potential uses, from helping self-driving cars read traffic signs to aid in diagnosing medical conditions in medical imaging systems.

For AI, deep learning has opened up a whole new world of possibilities because it can see highly complicated connections in data. The area of AI is rapidly developing and expanding. New ground-breaking applications and game-changing breakthroughs that will completely revolutionize how we use and benefit from AI are on the horizon.

Getting to Know Large Language Models (LLMs)

Switching gears a little bit, the development of LLMs, or large language models, is one of the most noticeable AI developments of recent years.

Unsupervised machine learning creates these models, which are then trained on huge amounts of text data to understand how people talk. This collection of texts includes papers, books, websites, and other types of written work.

During their training phase, LLMs sift through countless millions of sentences to find meaningful connections between concepts. Through this effort, these models will be able to respond when prompted that are remarkably similar to human language.

Before delving into the specifics of LLM training, it's essential to grasp the fact that these models set out to learn the full breadth of human knowledge in written form, picking up on subtleties of language and learning to comprehend the complexities of human communication in their natural settings. They understand the connections between words and phrases by reading a lot of text, so their answers make sense and are appropriate for the given context.

Among the most well-known LLMs is GPT-3.5, which serves as the foundation upon which ChatGPT was developed. It's lauded for its exceptional language-generating abilities. Besides that, there's the vast GPT-4, the biggest LLM ever made (Gothankar, 2023). Text created by these algorithms is often indistinguishable from that written by a person. One of the most formidable rivals in the LLM space is Google's LaMDA, the second-largest LLM. Although it takes a slightly different tack, its ultimate goal is the same: to understand and produce language that is indistinguishable from human beings.

Conversational AI

One application of LLMs, conversational AI, is an interesting area because it lets people and computers talk to each other. The designers of these systems carefully made them able to have conversations, just like people do. They can understand what users are saying and respond in a way that makes sense. Understanding and responding to human language in a way that is natural and conversational is the holy grail of AI, and natural language processing is at the center of this field.

There are different forms of conversational AI, each one meant to provide a different user experience. A well-known example is Google Bard, the leader in the field of robots. These chatbots are proficient in holding text-based conversations in real-time, answering questions, and resolving issues without the user lifting a finger.

Conversational AI relies heavily on natural language processing. Algorithms in these systems can parse phrases, understand context, and identify intent to mimic the natural flow and intuitive nature of human speech. Conversational AI is constantly growing and changing. These algorithms are getting better and better as time goes on, improving their ability to understand what's going on in a given situation, recognizing nuances in language, and providing correct, personalized solutions.

Key Takeaways

- AI was once the stuff of science fiction, but it powers many useful technologies we rely on daily.
- AI's foundational technologies—deep learning, machine learning, and neural networks—allow it to recognize and respond to complex patterns and make independent judgments.
- AI's potential is constantly changing. For example, Large Language Models (LLMs) can understand and produce language that sounds like human speech. Conversational AI systems let people talk to computers naturally.

We'll learn more about how AI is impacting education as we read this book. We'll go into how AI can be used to improve classroom practices and pique students' interest in learning. In subsequent chapters, we'll delve deeper into the AI education revolution and explore the astounding opportunities it presents for reforming the field.

Chapter 2
AI Revolution in Education

Have you ever imagined having an AI-powered teaching helper who could adapt to the needs of each student and grade their work without missing a beat? What if there was a way for schools to know which students needed extra help and which had their own distinct learning methods?

It's not hard to imagine a world where AI plays a vital role in the classroom— where teachers don't have to spend as much time on planning or paperwork, so they can spend more time doing what they do best: motivating and leading their students. These aren't predictions for the future; great things are happening now in the world of teaching, but first, let's understand how we got here.

In this chapter, we'll explore the history of AI in education, starting with an AI system named Eliza that was created in the 1960s up to the ever-changing environment of AI's effect on classrooms today, where the lines between disciplines are blurring at an unprecedented rate.

AI in Academics: A Journey Through Time and Technology

Academically speaking, AI has made great strides in a very short time. Let's briefly look at the most critical steps that AI has taken in the field of education.

The Early Years of AI

AI first entered the classroom in the 1960s, when computer technology was only getting started. Scholars at MIT with foresight, including Joseph Weizenbaum, launched initiatives that would change the face of learning forever.

Among the earliest watershed moments was their development and eventual debut of ELIZA. ELIZA was a rudimentary AI system that used natural language processing to converse with a person via computer. As it talked, ELIZA was more than just software; it showed what could be possible.

While this AI was initially developed in the educational setting during this era, it wasn't until the turn of the century that AI was leveraged as a tool for teaching and learning in schools.

The Millennium Learning Boom (2000-2009)

With the start of the new century came significant changes in how people learned. Online education was made possible by digital learning platforms, allowing teachers to reach more students. A fascinating subtheme that arose was virtual reality (VR), which gave students access to novel educational environments and changed their lively interactions with teachers.

In the early stages of its impact on the classroom, VR took students to interactive 3D representations of made-up worlds. Teachers rapidly saw the benefits of VR for increasing students' interest in and ability to remember lessons. It also highlighted the need for teachers to have a firm grasp of digital literacy and virtual identities before implementing these tools successfully in the classroom.

The Revolution of Intelligent Tutoring Systems, Student Profiling and Learning Analytics (2010–2018)

The introduction of ITSs, or Intelligent Tutoring Systems, was a significant breakthrough during this time. These cutting-edge AI products were planned to provide individualized instruction and critique to each learner, frequently with little to no human involvement. In order to make learning better and faster, these systems used AI tools such as knowledge bases, student models, user interfaces, and teaching modules.

Arguably, the most well-known and influential application of machine learning to personalized instruction is Jill Watson, an intelligent instructor created at Georgia Tech (Hardman, 2023). When a student uses Jill Watson, the system keeps track of how well they do on quizzes and how quickly they finish tasks, among other metrics. Then, this information is used to teach a reinforcement learning program how to figure out which learning activities or help will work best for each student.

The ability of intelligent tutoring systems like Jill Watson to provide personalized help and feedback to each student was a significant advantage, especially in big classrooms where it might be challenging for the instructor to give individualized attention to each learner.

Education went through a profound change during this time also because models emerged for creating student profiles. These models were very helpful in figuring out which students excelled in the classroom, and which ones needed more help.

Profiling models for pupils used data and complex algorithms to generate in-depth profiles of each student. These profiles covered various characteristics, from a person's preferred learning style and existing strengths to the areas where they could benefit from reinforcement. Instructors could make better decisions about their teaching methods and adjustments with more information about each student's academic journey.

Another helpful tool was learning analytics, which involved gathering and analyzing information about students to learn essential things about their growth and performance. When teachers could see patterns in their students' progress in real-time, they could adapt their lessons accordingly. This data-driven method had a considerable impact on education, making the classroom more flexible and dynamic.

From Teacher-Centered to Learner-Centered (2019–Present)

Recent years have seen a dramatic transition in the educational system, one that places more emphasis on the student rather than the teacher. AI was essential in this shift since it considered individual differences among students. By adapting to each student's preferred method of instruction, AI technologies quickly earned a place among teachers' most trusted assistants.

This historical and technological trek shows how AI has progressed from its early days in the classroom in the 1960s to its current role as a driving force behind tailor-made, student-centric instruction.

Learning analytics has also hit a mature stage in education, contributing to this shift. With data-driven ideas that change the way we teach and learn, this evolution gives teachers and institutions more power. Institutions make the best use of their resources to improve the learning process as a whole, making the ecosystem more responsive and student-centered. This change shows how powerful data can be in changing the way we learn.

Today's Use of AI in Classrooms

The possibilities today are truly exceptional, and they promise a myriad of ways to improve the learning process. Although AI's use in education is still in its infancy, it has already shown promising results that indicate favorably for the future of education. As we explore this dynamic field, it becomes clear that AI is more than a fleeting trend; it is a powerful tool that has the potential to enhance the educational experiences of both teachers and students. With the help of AI, the way we think about education is about to undergo a radical transformation.

Let's start this journey by discussing some of the ways AI could impact education. AI has many exciting applications in the classroom, and exploring them is an adventure that yields many positive results for students and teachers alike.

Automation

When it comes to saving time and effort, automation in education is not limited to only the classroom. Think about all the labor that goes into checking for and correcting instances of plagiarism and grading student assignments. Teachers can quickly spot trends in their students' performance with the help of machine learning and natural language processing, which helps them make the best use of their teaching methods.

Collaboration

Another way AI is changing schooling is by making it easier for people to work together. It goes beyond simple individual education to improve institutional collaboration. Students can learn more about their subjects in depth through VR and augmented reality (AR), which also encourages them to collaborate. These technologies make the surroundings more exciting and interactive, encouraging people to learn together. In addition, AI can be integrated with social networking platforms, allowing students to interact with one another and their teachers in a virtual learning environment, thus fostering greater online collaboration and information sharing.

Personalization

In addition, AI can tailor each student's learning experience to their unique needs. Below, we'll go into more depth on this topic.

Example Uses of AI in Education

Adaptive Learning - AI plays a critical role in education by helping to design individualized lessons. The most up-to-date versions of these tools use sophisticated machine learning methods to check how well students are doing and adjust their learning activities as needed. Nothing is more important than changing the level of difficulty, the material, and the pace of the lessons to meet the needs of each student.

When it comes to improving student achievement, the idea of personalized learning has a lot of promise. Students are free to learn at their own pace, creating an atmosphere free from frustration and boredom.O

Controlling Class Behavior - A personalized learning experience depends on how well students can behave in the classroom. We do know, though, that this is easier said than done, which is why teachers have to spend a lot of time keeping things in order. Face identification, behavior prediction algorithms, and automatic feedback systems are just a few examples of how AI is helping teachers upgrade their classrooms so their pupils can focus on what they're supposed to be doing there: learning.

Training Young Minds - When it comes to students from different social backgrounds, educational differences often start when they are very young. Low-income families are often at a loss because their pupils don't have the same developmental skills as children from wealthier families when they start school.

Many low-income schools, for instance, have yet to realize the ideal of installing high-tech audio-visual equipment like SmartBoards. But AI is a ray of hope, one that can bridge these gaps. The learning gap is narrowed as teachers are able to provide more individualized instruction to their students through engaging materials.

Overcoming Learning Barriers - AI can help pupils who have unique needs in the classroom. Voice recognition and speech synthesis are two examples of how AI technologies are helping people with communication challenges overcome obstacles to more effective expression.

Students with impairments can benefit from these tools because they employ visuals and simulations to help them better understand the course material. Additionally, AI's ability to improve one-on-one teaching is truly revolutionary, providing scalability that can completely transform training programs.

Scheduling - Ensuring all students have equal access to classes, learning materials, and specific teaching time is another important task. Smarter scheduling helps instructors keep their jobs because it frees them up to design more effective lessons and spend more time with their families, both of which contribute to a lower teacher turnover rate. Using AI-driven scheduling algorithms speeds up the process of developing schedules that are a good fit for these goals.

Facility Administration - It's nothing new for education managers to spend a lot of time overseeing facility management. They have to make sure that schools are always clean and well taken care of. AI's strengths, especially in picture recognition, make it possible to automate these processes. It becomes easier to keep an eye on how much water and energy are being used while still controlling heating systems. The use of AI to fine-tune HVAC systems is a further step toward streamlined building management.

Preparing Lessons - One other important area where AI might play a role is in educational materials. It's a useful tool for educators looking to make and exchange content. Content recommender systems driven by AI, for instance, can help educators in meeting the individualized learning requirements of their pupils. Plus, machine learning can help educators zero in on the methods that have proven to yield the best results in the classroom, consequently improving their own ways of teaching.

Language Learning - Foreign language classes are often some of the hardest classes for students to do well in. Students have to learn a whole new set of words and language rules all the time, no matter how well they learn other things.

Learners of a language can benefit from AI-enhanced language-learning algorithms because of the tailored feedback they provide. To further facilitate cross-cultural communication, AI can now use natural language processing to offer quick translation services.

Exam Studying - Although we may agree that multiple-choice exams have their flaws, it is undeniable that they play an important role in the educational process. Many students, though, have trouble with standardized tests. So, it might be challenging for educators to give these students the required help.

Students can raise their test scores by learning AI's conceptual underpinnings. It gives you comments and practice questions that are specific to you. With the help of AI's machine learning, deep learning, and natural language processing capabilities, students can acquire the knowledge and abilities necessary to do well on any examination.

Assessment - Students can be evaluated in a variety of ways besides standardized tests. The right or wrong response matters, to be sure, but there are other factors at play when assessing a student's grasp of a subject. A lot of new assessment tools and AI-powered adaptive learning systems can help teachers learn more about how their students do in class.

LMS—Learning Management System - A well-rounded and intuitive learning management system is the foundation of any effective educational program. It is the bedrock of any respected learning institution. Students can interact with each other and the teacher in a more meaningful way through the use of a learning management system. Much of the technology used in schools is AI, which helps students keep track of their work and stay organized.

Management of Staff Availability and Schedules - When it comes to school staff, management tools powered by AI are changing how schools work. These methods can make it easier for teachers to plan their lessons. On top of that, they help administrators find teacher openings and fill them. There are times when not having enough teachers can make it harder to learn. For school staff to stay prepared and get work done, they need useful tools.

Gamification to Get Students More Involved - Gamification methods can make learning much more fun. It helps students get involved, stay motivated, and make friends. Teachers can make any subject more engaging for students to learn by using tools like AR and VR.

Gamification could also be used in many different types of school settings. Education classes for young children, middle and high school, and professional training are all included. We can teach students new things through games or use games as tests to see how they're doing.

Cybersecurity - In today's world, the scope of educational solutions goes far beyond the lecture hall. Universities and colleges need to have strong computer security systems. Using AI, schools can monitor for and stop incidents of cyberbullying and other forms of online harassment. AI can be used to do things like check schools for common hacking methods and loopholes. This allows them to prevent any possible attackers from getting the upper hand.

Growth as a Professional - AI is being utilized to advise educators on how to improve their teaching methods in a variety of subject areas in the context of professional development. Along with that, it can give them feedback in real-time to help them get better at training.

Peace of Mind and Safety - With the help of new technology, schools are becoming safer and more private. AI can be used to help schools come up with new ways to keep students safe. When put into place, these systems can identify risks long before they lead to any real trouble. Several educational institutions are using data analytics software to help spot students facing challenges that could put themselves or other students at risk. This enables them to receive the help they need to thrive academically and in life.

Looking at Metrics for Student Success - When it comes to teaching tools, standard grade levels are quickly going out of style. AI has made it possible for teachers to judge a student's overall success based on how well they know certain things. These metrics can also help teachers determine where their students have gaps in knowledge.

Research in Schools - A person can still learn after they graduate. AI is now being used to guide academic study at many universities. Insights and facts that can help researchers do better work can be found easily.

Connected Campuses - Slowly but steadily, walls are coming down between K-12 and higher education. Connected campuses that facilitate resource sharing among several parties are being built with the use of AI by many institutions today. For example, schools and colleges can now work together on projects that help students that serve both.

Accessibility in the Classroom - All students, regardless of their background, abilities, or resources, should have equal access to educational opportunities. Artificial intelligence can make learning accessible to all pupils. It has the potential to generate novel learning models that are specific to each student. It can do this while reducing the time and money required to produce one-of-a-kind educational resources.

Automatic Learning Instruction - Lastly, personalized learning plans are a benefit to all students. AI can help teachers ensure that each student's lessons are a good fit for their individual learning needs by looking at each student's skills and preferences. Students can benefit from this in the classroom, in their future careers, and their personal lives.

Key Takeaways

This chapter explored the history of AI in the classroom, from its earliest attempts to the present day.

- Early AI systems, such as ELIZA, were created in the 1960s by pioneers like Joseph Weizenbaum.
- AI makes individualized education possible by tailoring lessons to each student.
- Students can get personalized help from Intelligent Tutoring Systems.
- Student profile and learning analytics from AI inform data-driven education.

Chapter 3
AI Tools for Education

As we look into how AI can be used in education, our navigation system leads us toward a future where learning and teaching will be transformed in ways that have never been seen before. It's been a long road that began when Alan Turing's bright mind developed a test for AI in the 1950s (Copeland, 2019). More than 70 years later, the small changes that started with that one idea have grown into a huge wave of new ideas that are changing the world of education.

In 2019, UNESCO boldly predicted that AI in education would accrue a hefty $6 billion in value (Malekos, 2023). Currently, the market study points to this field being worth an astonishing $20 billion by 2027 (Inc, 2021). What seemed like a dreamy prediction at one point is now becoming a reality.

Do People Think AI Should be Used in Schools?

A survey by Common Sense Media has revealed that individuals aged 12-18 are more tech-savvy than their parents when it comes to understanding AI. The study found that 58% of adolescents and preteens have used ChatGPT, an AI-driven application that can answer questions, compose essays on Shakespearean plays, and even generate legal memos that appear astonishingly analogous to what a human can do. However, only 30% of parents have actually used the tool, and just roughly 30% of them are familiar with ChatGPT.

The study also found that while 50% of students aged 12-18 reported using ChatGPT for educational purposes, only 26% of parents did the same. However, both parents and children express curiosity about AI capabilities that could improve educational outcomes, with almost 83% of guardians and 92% of pupils being interested.

Parents make up 68% of those who think AI programs will improve education, while students make up 86%. However, almost half of the teachers who answered a recent poll said AI would make teaching and learning worse or more difficult five years from now. About a quarter (27%) think that the effects of AI will be beneficial or perhaps overwhelmingly positive. Despite widespread optimism about AI's potential benefits, both parents and children are aware of the serious risks that the technology poses.

Many parents and students worry that children might depend too much on smartphones and computers, or use technology to cheat. Moreover, half of all children and their parents believe that schools should establish policies on the implementation of AI in the classroom.

Exploring the Benefits and Drawbacks of AI in the Classroom

AI has the power to change and open up education, and it could also create new problems. Additionally, like other technologies, it has the potential to be used with both good and bad intentions, so it's critical to approach it with some caution. Let's dig into some of AI's benefits and potential drawbacks.

The Benefits

While there are neverending possibilities that arise when we integrate AI into the classroom, there are three key benefits we will discuss here:

Quality, Universal Access to Learning: Too often, what students can learn is restricted by what teachers can do and when they can do it. Technology based on AI has the potential to level the educational playing field for students with cognitive or neurological impairments. One way that AI can help students who are hard of hearing or who don't speak English as their first language is through immediate transcription and content adaptation.

Lightening the Mental Load: By lightening students' mental loads, we can help them zero in on what really matters, gain instant access to the data they need, and go through coursework more quickly.

Learning Tailored to Each Student: You can make a unique learning experience for each student by using AI tools to look at data about their preferred learning style, tempo, and other factors. Since not every student learns in a similar way or at a comparable pace, AI can facilitate the learning process by adapting the content to the individual's unique characteristics.

AI is like having a best friend by your side; it will help you become more knowledgeable and productive than ever before. Human intelligence will not be replaced; rather, it will be supplemented. With AI on your side, you can transform the way you teach.

The Drawbacks

So, while there are many benefits to incorporating AI into the classroom, there are also some caveats and risks to consider. The Future of Life Institute published an open letter in which some of our generation's best brains called for a halt to AI research and development (Future of Life Institute, 2023). Here's why:

Overload of Content: Overloading young minds with too much information is one of the biggest problems that AI could cause. People constantly exposed to such a large amount of content may get tired and lose motivation, which can hurt their academic success.

The End of Critical Thinking: Today's information-packed world makes analytical thinking more important than ever. One risk of using AI in education is that it could make people less critical thinkers who take in knowledge without checking to see if it's true. Especially in this day and age, when false information travels at what seems like the speed of light, this poses a serious threat to society at large.

Truth and Lies in Algorithms: When AI algorithms are trained on data that isn't representative of the whole, they can become biased, which is an important issue. This prejudice may lead to unfair treatment of some student populations through wrong evaluations, inappropriate suggestions, or unsuitable content.

Safety and Privacy of Data: Student privacy and data security are two issues that come up when discussing the use of AI in the classroom because of the volume of data that must be collected and analyzed. The only way to keep this kind of information safe is via strict administration.

Less Human Interaction: AI has the potential to improve education by providing more individualized feedback and assistance, but it cannot be a substitute for the value that a human teacher brings. Students may feel alienated from their friends and teachers if they rely too much on AI, preventing them from gaining important social and emotional skills.

Legal and Ethical Issues: Using AI in schools brings up moral and legal issues. Such concerns include unfair algorithms, data security, who owns the content, and openness. Institutions of higher learning and organizations providing professional development must tread cautiously around these challenges when they adopt AI-based solutions.

It is worth noting that, while there are many potential risks and drawbacks to incorporating AI into the educational environment, many of the concerns mentioned above can and are being addressed through policy and regulation.

Developing an AI-Driven Learning Environment

The rapid advancement of AI technology is predicted to alter the educational landscape completely, turning classrooms into AI-driven educational institutions. The way teachers do their jobs and the roles they play could evolve a lot as a result. Let's look at a few possible outcomes:

- Technology will be used heavily to help in the planning and drafting of curriculum and content prototyping (the creation of drafts, outlines, etc.).
- Creating course materials won't be the same anymore. To save time and effort, AI will be used to develop things like homework assignments, lecture notes, handouts, and even presentations.
- Creative roadblocks will be eliminated. When you sit down to write, do you ever dread staring at a blank page? If you get stuck when writing, using an autocomplete feature or an AI writing tool will get you back on track and writing again.
- This shift means teaching students to think critically will become a priority at all educational levels.
- As a teacher, one of your least favorite activities could be reading through and objectively rating stacks of student writing for course grades. Soon, we might have AI to help us with this job.
- AI will help with every part of the classroom experience, from generating test questions to grading papers and providing customizable feedback to students.
- Rather than wasting time and energy on routine activities, both the instructor and students will be able to focus on more substantive learning.

There are already existing AI tools that can help you and your peers achieve many of these outcomes. However, many aren't convinced yet that they should be using them. We are just in the beginning stages of integrating AI into the educational setting. As a reader of this book, you are truly a pioneer.

In future classrooms driven by AI, teachers will have to learn new ways of teaching, as well as new skills and abilities. While the tactics may shift, the educator's essential role of assisting students to learn and develop won't change.

What Does AI Integration in Schools Look Like?

Over the past few years, AI has transcended being just a science fiction concept to becoming a tangible reality that is progressively becoming more common in our daily lives. The question of when AI will become ubiquitous has now changed to a matter of how soon. The widespread utilization of AI in various fields has significantly impacted K-12 schools. A few key aspects are particularly important for academic institutions to take into consideration:

Firstly, schools can incorporate the use of existing AI solutions to enhance different aspects of their operations. AI has multiple applications, from improving student performance in class to making networks safer and easier to monitor. We will discuss these at length in later chapters and provide examples of some technologies you can use.

Secondly, it is crucial for students to learn how AI works. They should not only know how to use AI systems but also how to create and manipulate them. K-12 schools should include lessons on AI since, according to some estimates, as many as one in five future workers will work with AI. For example, in Pennsylvania's Montour School District, students learn about how machine learning works by using tablets and virtual assistants like Alexa and Google Home. School leaders must carefully plan and implement AI for it to work efficiently in the classroom.

To optimize scarce resources, AI can serve as a multipurpose digital assistant to ease the workload of K-12 teachers and administrators. However, personalization requires a significant amount of effort, and AI can be of assistance in this regard. Apple's AI-powered teaching assistants and mobile apps modify course materials based on student responses so that teachers can concentrate on the more personalized aspects of teaching.

AI also plays a pivotal role in creating safer learning environments in schools. For instance, GoGuardian's content surveillance software, which uses machine learning, puts suspicious internet searches into perspective and has been implemented in the Putnam County School District. Mental health professionals can quickly identify and prevent searches related to potential harm and self-harm utilizing this technology.

Currently Available AI Systems and Tools

AI tools have been proven to give teachers more time for instruction and less time spent on paperwork. These tools are not meant to replace teachers, but rather to free them up to devote more time to their students. With the rapid expansion of AI in schools, a multibillion-dollar industry has been created around the world. This growth can be attributed to the many ways in which AI can enhance the teaching and learning experience. Many businesses are investing in the development of AI technologies to further this evolution. Let's explore ten well-known AI-powered learning resources.

A Chatbot Named Ivy

The chatbot AI solutions developed by Ivy are specifically designed to assist with a wide range of tasks unique to higher education institutions, including but not limited to admissions, registration, billing, and recruitment. All the information a student needs to know about paying for college, including how to get financial aid, can be found on Ivy. It also provides department-specific chatbots for use within universities.

Cognii

Cognii, headquartered in Boston, develops AI-powered products for use in educational settings ranging from kindergarten through university, as well as in corporate training. Its conversational AI-powered learning assistant guides students through formulating free-form answers, honed critical thinking, and immediate, individualized feedback and instruction.

Fetchy

Fetchy is an AI-powered tool explicitly designed for teachers that streamlines everything from class planning to newsletter and email creation. Because it allows teachers to choose the parameters under which their language is generated, it is a valuable tool for improving efficiency and making more well-informed decisions.

The Dragon Speech Recognition System by Nuance

Nuance, headquartered in Boston, MA, develops speech recognition software that can transcribe at speeds of up to 160 words per minute (MurfResources, 2023). It lets you navigate documents with spoken words, which makes it a must-have for students with accessibility needs. The dictation function can create 99% accurate lesson plans, syllabi, and worksheets.

Knowji

Knowji is an interactive multimedia dictionary for students of foreign languages. The algorithm uses spaced repetition to keep tabs on how far along learners are with a word and how close they are to forgetting it. Many different learning modes, personalization options, and illustrative materials like pictures and model sentences are only a few of the features.

Querium

The AI platform developed by Querium is geared toward facilitating students' development of STEM competencies. It helps you learn better and faster by giving you guided lessons and step-by-step help. Through AI research, teachers can learn more about how their students learn and where they can improve.

Plaito

Plaito is a digital coach that helps students with their writing, discussions, and group projects. This AI application combines the advantages of one-on-one tutoring by creating individualized lessons for each student. It's fun to use, can be used with various languages, and can help you form good language-learning habits with its game-like elements and persistent prompts.

Century Tech

London-based Century Tech uses AI and cognitive sciences to make custom lesson plans for each student. These strategies lighten the pressure on teachers while delivering valuable data insights. Century Tech keeps track of each student's progress, finds gaps in their knowledge, and gives each student personalized study suggestions and comments.

Carnegie Learning Platforms

Carnegie Learning is a learning platform that uses machine learning and AI to help students in high school and college. These online resources provide a personalized learning experience that is reminiscent of human teachers, and they cover a wide range of subjects, including mathematics, literacy, and foreign languages. They give you information you can use to manage your classroom better. Carnegie Learning's AI-based teaching apps have won awards.

Key Takeaways

- AI has changed quickly and is predicted to be a $20 billion business in education by 2027, having a significant effect on how we teach and learn.
- It is essential to take a balanced view of AI in education, considering its possible pros and cons, such as privacy issues and too much content.
- For schools to use AI responsibly, they need to plan carefully, consider ethics, and teach students to use AI.

Chapter 4
ChatGPT for Curriculum Design

As individuals who care about their students' success, teachers are always trying to keep them interested and motivated. Creating a curriculum that does more than just teach facts but also gets the class excited to learn is a delicate ballet that requires careful planning. However, teachers in the modern era are learning to dance with a new partner: AI.

With a whiteboard in hand, an excited teacher stands in front of a class full of eager pupils. The new school year has begun, and the teacher's goal is crystal clear: to design a curriculum of study that will pique the class' interests and propel them forward on a journey of discovery that will last throughout the academic year. Although, as the days pass, the creative well starts to dry up. It's hard for the teacher to create a fun, educational, and interesting lesson plan for the hungry minds in their care. The challenge is real and thousands of teachers can relate to this experience.

Join me as we investigate how AI might inspire and motivate Educators to create new and engaging lessons for their students. The purpose of this chapter is clear: to provide readers with the skills they need to make the most of AI resources to improve their learning environments.

Trends in Curriculum Development

Curriculum development issues and trends are the problems and shifts that affect the making and using of instructional plans. Some of the most pressing concerns and emerging tendencies in course design are:

Technological Integration: Since technology is always improving, it should be a part of the school curriculum to prepare students for the future job market. There is a growing movement in curriculum development called "inclusive education," which means ensuring that all students, even those with disabilities or from different backgrounds, can participate in the lessons.

Personalization: The move toward personalized learning is picking up speed. This type of learning lets students make it fit their own wants and interests.

Global education: An addition in curriculum development is to prepare children for a global society. Teaching language, cultural awareness, and global problems are all ways to address this. More and more people are realizing how important it is to meet students' social and emotional needs, so curriculum designers are adding social-emotional learning to their lessons.

One of the fastest-growing movements in curriculum design is environmental education, which emphasizes the importance of informing students about environmental problems and encouraging them to adopt sustainable lifestyles.

Career readiness: Getting students ready for their future careers is very important, and new courses are being made that concentrate on job expertise, internships, and trade training. When it comes to ensuring the curriculum fulfills its goals and objectives, assessing students' learning outcomes and evaluating them correctly is critical.

Curriculum Designing and ChatGPT

ChatGPT's useful features set it apart as a powerful tool for the classroom. It fits naturally into several critical facets of the learning process, including content generation, curation, and individualized learning pathways.

ChatGPT is unparalleled in its ability to generate insightful and entertaining content. This AI-powered helper makes making lesson plans, worksheets, and educational articles easier. What makes it unique is that it can adapt the material to meet students' different wants and needs. This ensures that learning stays interesting and useful for students at all levels.

ChatGPT is just as useful for content curation as any other tool. Finding and organizing training materials is made much easier by its ability to give clear, concise answers to questions. This feature lets users get explanations, summaries, or relevant information on a lot of different topics. This makes it easier to choose and put together educational materials.

In addition, ChatGPT helps in creating more dynamic educational materials. It paves the way for more personalized education by allowing users to make their own quizzes, flashcards, and interactive activities.

ChatGPT's conversational style is one of its most notable qualities. Because of this special quality, it can have a two-way conversation with students and learn about their individual interests, ambitions, and skill levels. ChatGPT can tailor instruction based on this knowledge. For example, it can change how difficult math problems are, suggest extra resources, and give step-by-step explanations depending on how the student is doing and what they say.

Along with this, ChatGPT changes how it talks to students to accommodate their different ways of learning. It recognizes that some people learn best through visuals, while others learn best through words on a page, ensuring that the generated material fits each student's unique way of learning by considering these needs.

When conducting research or curating content, ChatGPT can be an invaluable tool for verifying facts, creating citations, and offering references to back up claims. In addition, ChatGPT's individualized learning paths might incorporate recommendations for supplemental readings, movies, or activities depending on a student's performance and areas of interest. This way of teaching promotes exploration and self-directed learning.

Last but not least, ChatGPT works with teachers to create in-depth learning paths that cover a wide range of subjects and levels of complexity. These learning paths give students an organized and personalized learning method that helps them reach their goals.

How Educators Can Leverage ChatGPT

Here's a close look at how educators have been using ChatGPT and how you can use it, too!

Suggesting Tough Conversations Through Role Play

Dr. Helen Crompton, a Professor of Instructional Technology at Old Dominion University, tells her graduate students in education to use ChatGPT to pretend to be someone else (OpenAI, 2023). For example, a debater's opponent may criticize their ideas, a job interviewer may ask leading questions and a manager's feedback style may vary. She believes students have a more nuanced and well-rounded understanding of their subject matter when exploring it in a conversation.

Using Course Materials to Design Quizzes, Exams, and Lessons

A Professor at Spain's Universidade da Corua, Fran Bellas, has endorsed using ChatGPT as a helpful tool for educators in developing tests, quizzes, and lessons (OpenAI, 2023). He recommends posting the course outline on ChatGPT and then asking for help creating new quizzes and lesson plans incorporating current events and cultural references. When Bellas wants to make sure the questions her professors write are appropriate for all pupils, regardless of ability, she uses ChatGPT to check for her.

Increasing Accessibility for Non-Native English Speakers

Dr. Anthony Kaziboni, the University of Johannesburg's Head of Research, instructs pupils who, for the most part, are not fluent in English (OpenAI, 2023). Kaziboni thinks that knowing English is incredibly helpful in the academic environment and that even minor grammar mistakes might prevent a student from being taken seriously. His class discussions, writing, and conversational English all benefit from his pupils' use of ChatGPT.

Critical Thinking Lessons for Students

Geetha Venugopal, an educator at the American International School in Chennai, India, teaches computer science to high school students and compares instructing them on using AI tools to instructing them on safe online behavior (OpenAI, 2023). While using ChatGPT, she reminds her students that the answers they receive may not always be reliable, encourages them to critically evaluate whether or not they should accept the response, and encourages them to double-check the information by consulting other primary sources. The objective is to get students to recognize the value of making a concerted effort to develop their unique critical thinking, problem-solving, and creative abilities daily.

What's the Scoop on ChatGPT?

Let's talk about the elephant in the room. You have heard about ChatGPT by now. But what exactly is this bot? If there were an AI equivalent of a unicorn, it would be this handy little software. With the help of AI and natural language processing, ChatGPT can transform your discussions into a scene from a futuristic film.

However, that's not all. This intelligent robot can assist you with more than just idle chatter. Want to send an email that will make your employer do a happy dance? ChatGPT has your back. What about finally getting that essay done that has been weighing on your mind? You have a new writing pal. ChatGPT can help you fix and optimize your code if you're a beginner programmer. Need to prioritize your to-do list? Look no further.

The best part? Anyone can use ChatGPT without paying a dime. ChatGPT Plus is a premium paid version that debuted in February for those who want to take things to the next level. The premium version of the tool uses OpenAI's most advanced language learning model to date, ChatGPT-4, which means higher quality responses. Premium users also get first dibs when the system is overloaded and bogged down by too many users. As of the writing of this book, demand for the premium version of ChatGPT is so high that there's a waitlist to sign up. That's how much of a game-changer this tool is; people are catching on quickly.

What is ChatGPT used for?

ChatGPT does a lot more than just provide answers to basic questions. ChatGPT can write essays, give in-depth artwork descriptions, generate AI-generated art prompts, engage in philosophical discussions, and even write code on your behalf.

The most helpful application for me is getting the chatbot to generate simple lists for things like traveling and grocery shopping and to-do lists that help me get more done each day. The range of outcomes is practically infinite.

Who's the Mastermind Behind ChatGPT?

Who exactly is the genius who conceived of this innovative solution? The answer is OpenAI - the superheroes of AI and research. ChatGPT was unveiled to the public on November 30, 2022, as reported by Ortiz in 2023. OpenAI has also developed Whisper, an automatic voice recognition system, and DALL-E 3, an artificially intelligent art creator that can produce images on demand.

Is ChatGPT available as an app?

To answer your question, ChatGPT has an official iOS and Android app. Beware of downloading any apps from the app store that claim to be linked with ChatGPT but are actually just clones of OpenAI's original software; these apps are easily distinguished by their lack of the trademark "ChatGPT" in the app's name.

Is there a free version of ChatGPT?

No matter what you plan on doing with ChatGPT—writing, coding, or anything else—it won't cost you a dime. Users can sign up for a monthly service that costs $20 per month. The paid subscription plan promises users extra benefits, like accessing GPT-4, having quicker responses, and connecting to the internet via plugins, even when the server is full.

Although the paid version promises access to the most recent version of the large language model (LLM), called GPT-4, and the internet, the free version is still a good choice for most because it has many of the same technical features.

So, how does ChatGPT actually work?

At the heart of how ChatGPT works is a complex neural network called the Transformer model. This model has a unique attention mechanism that allows it to think about how each word or token fits into the larger picture of the sentence or text. By doing so, ChatGPT can better comprehend questions and provide meaningful answers by focusing on the right words and phrases.

To train ChatGPT, a massive dataset of online text corpus is used to learn grammar, syntax, and linguistic nuance. ChatGPT separates it into individual words and phrases called tokens when you type in a question or text. Then, it goes through these tokens one at a time, guessing the next token in the order based on the information given. ChatGPT's generates answers with some degree of uncertainty due to its use of probabilistic generation. It creates words based on random chance, and based on the current situation, it determines which of several predicted tokens is the most likely to be used next.

Because ChatGPT remembers what has been said previously, it can answer follow-up questions and logically explain its actions throughout the conversation. It recalls your past conversations to make sure the current one makes sense. Also, ChatGPT's ability to generate material in a given job or topic can be "fine-tuned" to improve its performance. This process requires more training on data specific to the job.

ChatGPT's parent company, OpenAI, has added moral standards to stop its bots from making offensive or improper comments. These principles aim to ensure that AI actions are consistent with human values. Finally, ChatGPT models are continually getting better through a process called "iteration." Feedback from users and real-world use are essential for improving the model's features and fixing its problems.

It's important to remember that ChatGPT doesn't have any innate knowledge and instead uses what it's learned. Fact-checking can be essential to avoid using incorrect or outdated information provided by ChatGPT. For instance, ChatGPT was last updated in April 2023, and if you were to ask it who the all-time leading scorer in the NBA is, it would tell you it's Kareem Abdul-Jabbar. But, many basketball fans could tell you that LeBron James overtook that position in February 2023.

Where does ChatGPT fall short?

ChatGPT has limited capabilities despite its appealing appearance. Users may need to rephrase inquiries several times before ChatGPT gets it. That's why more precise and detailed prompts are better. Its responses, which sometimes sound plausible but make little practical sense or are overly verbose, are significant drawbacks. This is becoming less common as ChatGPT's language model becomes more sophisticated.

It may return unintended results because the model does not bother to inquire for clarification on unclear questions. Some people think these programs are only brilliant at arranging words in a way that makes statistical sense. Still, they don't grasp what's being said or whether their claims are valid.

Another significant drawback has been that ChatGPT only has data through 2021. The chatbot is unaware of the developments in the world since then. Lastly, the answers provided by ChatGPT are not accompanied by any citations.

However, these two issues have been mostly resolved thanks to ChatGPT's adoption of Bing as its primary search engine. ChatGPT can now index the web and offer citations thanks to a Bing plugin. Though currently only available to ChatGPT Plus members, the Bing plugin will soon be available to everyone.

Getting Started With ChatGPT

Joining the AI club is easy if you can access a computer and the internet. To sign up for OpenAI, go to chat.openai.com and follow the prompts to create a new account. Once you have logged in, you can start having conversations using ChatGPT. You are welcome to ask as many questions as you like.

But how can you fully leverage this AI supercomputer? Let's break it down into simple steps. This guide will help you whether you are new to AI or already have some experience.

Step 1: Open ChatGPT

As mentioned, first, you must sign up and log in to ChatGPT. For this, you can use any standard web browser or, if available, a specialized app. You can navigate to the login page by going to chat.openai.com. From there, follow the prompts to create an account and login.

Step 2: Define Your Objective

For what reason have you stumbled upon chatGPT? Figure out your goal before you start. Want to learn how to write killer material, get assistance with your research, or develop unique ways to impress your students? Having a clear idea of where you want to go is essential. This will help you tell ChatGPT exactly what you need it to do for you.

Step 3: Make Clear and Direct Prompts

It's recommended to have a clear plan when communicating with ChatGPT. It's best to be direct and concise when asking for help or guidance. For example, if you need assistance creating a lesson plan, a prompt such as "Assist me in creating a great lesson plan for sixth-grade students on the topic of the solar system" would be suitable.

If you're unsure where to start, try using a prompt such as "I'm a first-grade teacher who needs help teaching reading. What are some good strategies to begin with?" ChatGPT will provide you with top-tier recommendations to help you achieve your goals.

Step 4: Make Changes and Work Together

You are the one who leads, and ChatGPT is just here to lend a helping hand. Once you receive a response, you can go back and provide more information to your initial prompt or suggest a follow-up idea. You can simply say, "You're on the right track, but I need more information" or "I like this, but can you add [SPECIFIC TOPIC] to the curriculum?" In the field of teaching, your knowledge is like a secret ingredient. To get the best results, combine it with ChatGPT. Writing effective prompts is a skill that gets better with practice, so please be patient with yourself.

Step 5: Include References

Be sure to give proper citations when conducting research. Make sure you give credit where it's due by using ChatGPT's resources. It's the equivalent of "thank you" in the academic world.

Other Tips to Get the Most Out of ChatGPT

Ensure Quality: Supervise ChatGPT closely to ensure that the content it produces meets your standards. It's a fancy piece of technology, but that shouldn't make you slack up on quality control.

Make a Feedback Loop: ChatGPT learns quickly but could benefit from some supervision. Kindly correct it or ask for clarification if it makes an error. It's like teaching a dog a trick but with fewer treats.

Protecting Personal Information: Let's keep this under wraps. Pay attention to data protection and privacy. In other words, you shouldn't provide any sensitive information with automated systems.

Continuous Learning: Ensure that you are up to date on the most recent trends in AI implementation in educational settings. As AI develops, you may find new methods to significantly enhance your classroom effectiveness. There's a good chance that by the time you read this, ChatGPT will have released new features that make the tool even better and more user-friendly.

Share and Collaborate: Now, don't take all the fun away from other people! Talk about your experiences and what you've learned using ChatGPT with your coworkers. Collaboration is key to success in any endeavor, but it is crucial in the academic environment.

Formulating Effective Prompts

Users can have more natural chats with their AI-powered chatbot when using clean and concise prompts. Carefully crafted prompts will help the model produce relevant results to your context, issue, or goal. Customizing and providing detailed prompts is a good way to make interactions with ChatGPT more accurate and useful. Here are a few examples of how to create top-notch prompts:

Question Types: Instead of asking general questions, ask questions tailored to your desired answers or information. For instance, if you want a more in-depth explanation of the greenhouse effect, you could ask, "Describe the greenhouse effect in detail."

Content-Based Framing: Include background information in your questions to help ChatGPT understand the purpose or context of your request. For example, you could begin by asking, "In the context of literature from the 19th century, can you explain the importance of the term 'Moby Dick?'"

Problem-Solving Tips: When you need help or suggestions, make your comments more specific by explaining the issue and asking for help. For instance, *"I'm having trouble managing my time. Can you come up with good ways to make it better?"*

Include the Level of Depth You Want: Say what level of depth you want in answers. You can state, *"Give a brief summary of quantum physics fundamentals,"* or, *"Provide a comprehensive examination of quantum entanglement."*

Connection to a Specific Field: If your talk is about a particular subject or field, structure your prompts in a way that fits that field. For example, say, *"In the context of biological sciences, describe the process of photosynthesis."*

Progressive Explanation: If ChatGPT's first answer isn't clear or needs more information, you can change the next questions to ask for more information or explanation on certain points.

Personalized Instruction: If you want to use ChatGPT for educational reasons, you can change the prompts to fit your goals. Customized suggestions ensure the model delivers information that supports your teaching and learning objectives.

Effective Versus Ineffective Prompts

Crafting compelling and instructive conversations with ChatGPT requires mastery of the art of effective prompt creation. To that end, you can consider the following guidelines:

Maintain Clarity and Specificity: When writing prompts, it is crucial to keep clarity and specificity. If your questions aren't clear, you'll get answers that aren't either clear or relevant. Be specific about the scope of your inquiry by outlining the exact topic or data you need. Make it clear to ChatGPT what you want it to do when you ask a question or make a request.

Example:

Ineffective Prompt: *"Tell me about science."*

Improved Prompt: *"Describe the basic concepts of photosynthesis in plants."*

Ask Open-Ended Questions: Conversations that are both interesting and educational benefit greatly from the use of open-ended questions. By asking these questions, they force ChatGPT to provide in-depth explanations beyond a simple "yes" or "no" answer. If you want to use this method successfully, frame your inquiries with "what," "how," and "why." These inquiry prompts are designed to elicit thoughtful, in-depth responses.

Example:

Ineffective Prompt: *"Is climate change real?"*

Improved Prompt: *"What are the main causes of climate change?"*

Give Context: Contextual questions are helpful when discussing specific topics or looking for in-depth answers. Start your prompts with some history, pertinent facts, or an introduction to set the stage. Providing ChatGPT with some background information will allow it to interpret your question better and provide you with precise answers.

45

Example:

Ineffective Prompt: *"What is the capital of France?"*

Improved Prompt: *"In the context of European capitals, can you name me the capital city of France?"*

Ask for Different Points of View: To encourage deep reflection and insightful conversations, you could ask ChatGPT to give different points of view on a matter. You can do this by requesting opposing arguments, arguments from both sides or other points of view. You may make the discussion more useful and engaging by pushing for a multifaceted analysis of the subject at hand.

Example:

Ineffective Prompt: *"Explain the benefits of renewable energy."*

Improved Prompt: *"Can you present justifications both in favor and against the utilization of renewable energy sources?"*

Ask for More Details: If you want to learn more, don't hesitate to ask ChatGPT to go into more detail about certain things. Make use of prompts that stately demand additional information. This method generates more in-depth responses, simplifying otherwise difficult topics.

Example:

Ineffective Prompt: *"Describe the concept of demand and supply."*

Improved Prompt: *"Please define the concept of supply and demand and elaborate on how it affects market prices."*

Ask for Both Explanations and Examples: If you want to help people understand better, use questions asking for explanations and real-life examples. ChatGPT can, for example, explain an idea and give you examples to go with it. This method makes abstract ideas more concrete and difficult-to-understand topics more approachable.

Example:

Ineffective Prompt: *"Explain the concept of inertia."*

Improved Prompt: *"Can you explain the concept of inertia and provide real-life examples where it is observed?"*

Ask Positively: The way you word your questions can greatly affect the quality of the answers you get. Rephrase requests positively rather than negatively. For instance, you could say "Please give a detailed explanation" instead of "Don't be brief." ChatGPT responds better to upbeat language, which results in more thorough and logically organized responses.

Example:

Ineffective Prompt: *"Don't be vague."*

Improved Prompt: *"Please give a full and detailed answer."*

Clear Up Any Doubts: If ChatGPT's answers aren't clear or are missing information, use the follow-up questions to get more information or explanation. This will keep the conversation on course and guarantee that you obtain information that is relevant to your needs.

Example:

Ineffective Prompt: *"Describe the function of enzymes."*

Improved Prompt: *"I'm curious about the several enzymes that play a role in digestion. Could you please elaborate?*

Test and Refine: Adaptability is essential when creating prompts. Have fun trying out different methods. ChatGPT can come up with various answers depending on how you phrase your questions. By trying out several approaches and seeing which ones work best, you can learn how to best elicit the data or insights you need.

Example:

Ineffective Prompt: *"Explain to me what you know about AI."*

Improved Prompt: *"I'm interested in learning more about how AI is changing the medical field. Share your thoughts on the progress and difficulties.*

Break Down Complex Ideas into a Series of Sequential Prompts: When working with complicated ideas, you might want to break them down into a number of sequential prompts. Ask simple questions first, then move on to more complex ones. This strategy is helpful in developing an organized, well-rounded comprehension of complex topics.

Example:

Ineffective Prompt: *"Explain the theory of relativity."*

Improved Prompt:

- *"Start with the fundamentals of Einstein's theory of relativity. Now, let's dig deeper into the concept of time dilation in the theory of relativity."*

Don't Use Biased Language: To avoid biased answers, ensure your prompts are objective. ChatGPT's comments will always be fair and unbiased if you use neutral and impartial language. This is especially important when teaching, researching, or checking facts.

Example:

Ineffective Prompt: *"Talk about how electric cars are better for the environment than gas guzzlers."*

Improved Prompt: *"Analyze the advantages and disadvantages of electric cars in comparison to traditional gasoline-powered vehicles."*

Ask for Citations or Sources: If you are studying or checking facts, you might want to ask ChatGPT to give you sources or citations for the information it gives you. This allows you to double-check the information's correctness and dependability.

Example:

Ineffective Prompt: *"Explain quantum mechanics."*

Improved Prompt: *"Provide credible sources to support your explanation of the fundamental principles of quantum mechanics."*

These in-depth explanations of the best ways to make prompts will help you get the most out of your time using ChatGPT, whether you're using it to learn, study, or solve problems.

Now, this is just the beginning of effective prompting, and becoming a prompt expert is beyond the scope of this book. But with some practice and trial and error, you can graduate to providing detailed and specific prompts that get you exactly where you want to go, like this:

"Create an engaging and educational curriculum for fifth graders to learn about the American Civil War, assuming no prior knowledge. Begin with a brief introduction that explains what a civil war is. Introduce the American Civil War as a major conflict in the United States during the mid-19th century. Explain in simple terms the two opposing sides.

Illustrate the basic causes of the war in an easy-to-understand manner, such as disagreements over states' rights and the issue of slavery. Include a map to show the Union and Confederate states. Present a few key events and battles in a simple timeline format without assuming any prior knowledge of these events. Introduce a few important leaders from both sides using basic descriptions and images, but focus more on their roles (like 'leader of the Union') rather than their historical significance.

Briefly mention the Emancipation Proclamation in simple terms, such as a declaration that ended slavery. Conclude with a simple overview of the war's end and its major outcomes, like the reunification of the United States and the abolition of slavery. Use straightforward language, colorful illustrations, and clear layouts to make the infographic easy to understand for someone who is just beginning to learn about the American Civil War."

Sound intimidating? It certainly can be, which leads to the ultimate prompt hack to fast-track your ChatGPT training:

Have ChatGPT Create the Prompt For You: There can be a steep learning curve to writing perfect prompts. One way to speed that up is to reverse engineer it using ChatGPT by having it create the prompt for you. Try this: *"Create an effective ChatGPT prompt that I can provide ChatGPT to help me create a curriculum for eleventh graders about human anatomy."*

Creating Curriculum and Lessons Using ChatGPT

These prompts cover a range of subjects and can serve as a foundation for educators to build their own curriculum and lesson plans using ChatGPT. They are designed to inspire creativity, critical thinking, and engagement in the classroom.

1. History Curriculum

"Develop a history curriculum for high school students, focusing on the causes and consequences of World War II. Include key events, primary source documents, and engaging activities to facilitate a deep understanding of the topic."

2. Science Lesson Plan

"Design a lesson plan for middle school students that explores the solar system and the planets. Include interactive activities, visual aids, and clear explanations to make the topic engaging and easy to grasp."

3. Language Learning Program

"Create a language learning program for beginners studying French. Develop a series of lessons that cover essential vocabulary, grammar rules, and practical conversational scenarios."

4. Mathematics Quiz

"Prepare a mathematics quiz for 8th-grade students on algebraic equations. Include various problem types, from basic to advanced, along with step-by-step solutions."

5. Environmental Science Project

"Propose an environmental science project for high school students investigating local pollution issues. Outline the research process, data collection methods, and potential solutions to the problem."

6. Literature Analysis Assignment

"Create an assignment for a literature class where students analyze a classic novel. Include prompts for character analysis, themes, and writing style critique, encouraging critical thinking and literary exploration."

7. Art History Lesson

"Design an art history lesson for middle school students, focusing on a specific art movement or period. Include images of key artworks and questions encouraging students to interpret and appreciate the art."

8. Geography Exploration

"Develop a geography exploration project for elementary school students. Choose a country and create activities involving learning about its culture, landmarks, and geography."

9. Creative Writing Prompts

"Provide a set of creative writing prompts for high school students. Encourage them to write short stories, poems, or essays on topics like time travel, dystopian worlds, or the impact of technology on society."

10. Ethical Dilemma Discussion

"Create an ethical dilemma discussion activity for a philosophy class. Present students with a moral dilemma and ask them to explore different ethical perspectives and justify their choices."

• • •

Additional Sample Prompts

Here are five additional sample prompts that can be used for designing curriculum:

Sample Prompt 1:

"Create a curriculum for a middle school geography class focusing on global cultures and diversity. Include interactive lessons, case studies, and assessments that foster students' appreciation for different cultures and their impact on the world."

Sample Prompt 2:

"Design a curriculum for a high school computer science course emphasizing coding and programming. Outline the progression of skills to teach, provide coding challenges, and recommend coding platforms or languages."

Sample Prompt 3:

"Develop a curriculum for a health education class for elementary students. Detail the included topics, such as nutrition, physical fitness, and personal hygiene, and suggest fun and informative activities to engage young learners."

Sample Prompt 4:

"Craft a curriculum for a creative writing workshop at the college level. Provide a syllabus that includes writing prompts, peer review guidelines, and expectations for developing students' writing skills."

Sample Prompt 5:

"Create an art history course curriculum for advanced high school students. Select a specific art movement or era, and outline the key artworks, artists, and themes to be studied. Suggest research projects and field trips to enhance students' understanding of the topic."

You can test ChatGPT with any of these questions, and it should return helpful and instructive answers. Additionally, with minor modifications, you can leverage these prompts to plan specific lessons and activities in your classroom. Remember that ChatGPT is *conversational AI*. After it responds to your initial prompt, you can talk back to it like a person and ask it to include or exclude specific topics.

Strategies for Problem-Solving using ChatGPT

Let's take a closer look at how ChatGPT's features can be used to address common problems in the classroom. ChatGPT has many features and tools that are meant to make teaching easier, make it easier to make content and make learning more personalized. Here are some of the most important characteristics and how they might be used to solve problems:

Generating Content and Customization

ChatGPT's ability to make content is a useful feature for teachers. It can help you design lessons, worksheets, and articles that are specifically for your students. ChatGPT's content production can help you save time while ensuring that your solutions are entertaining and successful for students of varying skill levels and learning styles.

Fast Answers and Explanations

If you have questions or need clarifications, ChatGPT can answer quickly and correctly. Both teachers and students can greatly benefit from this addition. Teachers can utilize it to help students better understand difficult ideas, and students can get instant responses to their questions.

Interactive Educational Resources

ChatGPT can help you make quizzes, flashcards, tasks, and other interactive learning resources. It can meet each learner's needs by tailoring these materials to their specific style of instruction. Teachers can use this to their advantage by creating interesting lessons that meet their students' requirements in various ways.

Adaptation to Different Learning Modes

ChatGPT can change how it talks to students because it knows that each student learns differently. Whether a student learns best through seeing, hearing, or reading, ChatGPT can adapt to their needs and make sure that the material it creates fits their specific way of learning.

Live Feedback and Assessment

ChatGPT offers immediate feedback on tasks and essays. Teachers can get real-time feedback on their students' progress, make appropriate adjustments, and provide more personalized help. It helps students see where they stand and where they may make changes, which is essential for their development.

Suggestions for Additional Material

As part of customized learning plans, ChatGPT can recommend additional resources including articles, videos, and exercises depending on a user's current and past interests and performance. This supports exploration outside of the core curriculum and pushes students to learn independently.

Structured Learning Experiences

Through teacher collaboration, ChatGPT can construct in-depth learning journeys covering a wide range of topics and levels of difficulty. These trips give students a well-rounded education through planned and tailored learning.

Key Takeaways

• AI has a wide range of language-related capabilities, including text generation, question answering, and more.

• ChatGPT allows users to participate by asking questions or providing prompts.

• The model's response is determined by the information in the prompt and the state of the system.

• When used effectively ChatGPT can be used as a catalyst to significantly boost efficiency and inspiration.

Shape the Future of Education: Make an Impact With Your Review

"Kindness is the golden chain by which society is bound together." -
Johann Wolfgang von Goethe

Just like AI has evolved from the stuff of sci-fi movies to becoming an indispensable ally in our daily lives, your insights can transform the way education is perceived and practiced. At ModernMind Publications, we believe in harnessing the power of AI to revolutionize learning, and your feedback is the key to this evolution.

Please spare a minute to leave a review and make an impact. Your words can help:

- Ignite a passion for learning in young minds.
- Make classrooms more dynamic and interactive.
- Inspire educators to adopt innovative teaching methods.

Please scan the QR code to share your experience.

Your review is more than feedback; it's a guidepost for the future of education with AI. Thank you for being a part of this transformative journey.

With gratitude,

ModernMind Publications

P.S. Share the AI learning revolution! Pass this book to those who can benefit from it. Let's advance education together.

Chapter 5
Enhancing Student Engagement with AI

Despite the ever-changing nature of today's classrooms, student engagement remains the single most important predictor of educational success. It's clear that when students are interested in learning, they do better in school. In this day and age, where information is readily available, keeping students interested in class has become very important.

We can no longer rely on the methods of teaching propagated by textbooks, memorization, and a lack of active participation from students. One-size-fits-all lectures and a set curriculum are becoming less and less effective at capturing students' attention and giving them a sense of agency. It typically results in students being unmotivated, having trouble making connections in the course material, and wishing for more engaging and individualized learning opportunities. Fortunately, AI is the key that can open the door to a new age in education.

According to the Center for Teaching and Learning at the University of Washington, getting students involved in their learning is crucial for getting the results that are wanted (University of Washington, n.d.). First, let's define student engagement and then discuss why it's so important.

Student Engagement: A Definition

The term "student engagement" refers to a broad spectrum of actions, routines, and interpersonal links that motivate and inspire students to take an invested interest in their education. Students who are engaged in their learning do not passively absorb information; rather, they take an active role in the process and are intrinsically motivated to succeed.

Students' engagement can be measured in more ways than just whether or not they pay attention in class or turn in their homework on time. There are mental, psychological, and behavioral dimensions to it. Students who are truly invested in their learning go above and beyond what is required of them in terms of their curiosity, depth of understanding, and emotional investment in the material.

Reasons Why Student Engagement Is Important

When it comes to learning, why is student involvement so critical? There are numerous explanations for this.

- One benefit is improved academic performance in areas such as critical thinking, problem-solving, and information retention among the student body. When students are engaged, they learn the content more thoroughly and acquire more transferable skills.
- Engaged students have a strong internal drive to learn and are more likely to stick with a task until they master it. Students who have well-defined educational goals and actively pursue them have more resilience in the face of challenges.
- Additionally, a classroom where students actively participate will have a warm and welcoming environment. A sense of community and safety is fostered when students know they are appreciated and cared for.
- Engaging in activities outside of school helps students acquire important life skills including communicating with others, working together to solve problems, and being flexible in new situations.
- Students who are actively involved in their learning are better equipped to handle the complexities and unknowns of the

working world. They develop into lifelong students and analytical thinkers who can handle the challenges of a dynamic world.

- Another benefit of engagement is that it helps with personal growth. It fosters a growth mentality by having students discover their passions, establish personal objectives, and work toward them.

Obstacles to Student Engagement

While teachers try to get their students more involved, they have to deal with a number of problems that can get in the way of learning. This section delves further into these challenges and provides insights into how to overcome them.

- One of the biggest problems in schools nowadays is a general lack of interest and effort from children. Teaching students who are unmotivated or uninterested might feel like an uphill battle.
- There is great diversity among students in terms of their learning styles and skills. Because of this variety, it may be difficult to involve all students properly.
- The Internet's distraction - in today's high-tech world, it's not uncommon for students to struggle with the allure of the Internet. Their attention can be taken away from learning by things like social media, tablets, and games.
- The information isn't relevant to the students' lives, which is a key factor in keeping their attention. Making the material relevant is a difficult task.
- Psychological and emotional aspects - Students' motivation greatly benefits from their emotional health. Negative feelings, worry, or anxiety can make it difficult to learn.
- A high number of students in a class can make it difficult to provide each student with the attention they need.

- The emphasis on standardized tests may take the shine off of learning and encourage students to sit on the sidelines rather than become involved.
- Autonomy and freedom are highly valued by students as they progress through their education. With traditional education, this autonomy is often neglected.

Connecting AI and Engagement

Student involvement is where AI in the classroom really shines. Educators can use AI-enabled tools and tactics to design engaging, personally tailored lessons that pique students' interests, encourage exploration, and yield immediate results.

How Can AI Tools Make Classrooms More Interesting?

Traditional teaching methods can be used with these AI-driven techniques to make the classroom more open and interesting. This helps students develop a wide range of skills and a strong desire to keep learning throughout their lives. Using some of the following forms of AI integration can assist educators in better engaging their students.

A.I. Chatbots as a Tool for Interactive Education

Conversational AI chatbots provide a lively environment for active learning, keeping students interested and involved. Students can be tested, given individual comments, and allowed to learn at their own pace. Access to an AI chatbot as needed allows for more mobility and sustained concentration outside of the typical classroom setting. Teachers can use these to make learning fun, encourage students to learn at their own pace, and check on their progress, hopefully inspiring students to love learning for a lifetime.

AI-Generated Content Versus Traditional Literature

Pairing traditional books with material made by AI can make learning more fun for students. Students should be taught to think critically about the answers that AI gives them compared to the information they find in books. This activity will help students develop their critical thinking abilities, evaluate the credibility of different sources of information, and understand the potential and limitations of AI. By bringing together books and AI technology, you can create a well-rounded and exciting learning environment to help your students succeed in and out of the classroom.

Check the Accuracy of Data Generated by AI

Involving students in evaluating AI-generated responses for topics covered in the course is another great way to increase student engagement. This activity helps students develop their capacity to think critically and evaluate the credibility of the content they encounter. Students can gain a deeper understanding of the material and practice applying classroom knowledge to real-world scenarios by checking the accuracy of AI-generated answers. Giving students more power through this method boosts their confidence and freedom as they learn.

Fostering Student Creativity and Engagement with ChatGPT

ChatGPT is a tool that can help you rekindle students' drive to learn. Teachers can use its flexibility and reactivity to their advantage by developing engaging, student-centered lessons.

As for student diversity, the flexibility of ChatGPT makes it a useful tool for a wide range of educational settings and situations. By doing so, teachers can better adapt lessons and activities to students' individual needs and preferences. This flexibility guarantees that all students, despite their individual differences, will be able to actively participate in the learning process.

Distractions have multiplied in number in the digital age. To compete with other online distractions, ChatGPT offers appealing digital companionship in the form of engaging interactions. It helps students avoid becoming sidetracked by internet distractions so they can concentrate on their studies.

For students to stay interested, things must be relevant. ChatGPT's extensive database of information allows it to conjure up relevant instances and applications from the real world. By providing relevant real-world examples, the curriculum becomes more relevant and accessible to students.

Large classes make it difficult to provide each student with adequate attention. The scalability of ChatGPT is especially helpful in these kinds of situations. Teachers can utilize it to scale up their ability to provide individualized support and resources to all of their students while also facilitating classroom conversations.

Standardized testing overwhelms the learner and takes away the element of fun. ChatGPT finds a middle ground between cramming for the test and learning the material thoroughly. It can supply students with sample questions, answers, and explanations to help them study for exams without compromising the quality of their education.

Many favor learning autonomy. Using ChatGPT, students can get the confidence to learn independently. Teachers foster students' critical thinking and curiosity by showing them how to use ChatGPT for individual study. They'll feel more invested in their schooling as a result of this.

ChatGPT is a dynamic, knowledgeable, and flexible platform that can be used in various settings to address a wide range of student engagement issues. As we go along, we'll discuss concrete ways in which teachers can use ChatGPT to improve classroom climate and help all students feel welcome and engaged.

Teachers are always on the lookout for fresh approaches to pique their students' interest and encourage them to participate in class to increase student engagement. ChatGPT's unique nature can help educators generate ideas to interest students, as we demonstrate here.

Promoting Creativity with ChatGPT

One of the coolest things about ChatGPT is that it can lead to a lot of different and creative answers. This is a great tool for teachers to use to encourage student innovation in the classroom. That is, ChatGPT can help you come up with creative ideas when you are planning a critical thinking exercise or an imaginative writing exercise. If you give ChatGPT a prompt or topic, it will come up with a ton of ideas that you can use to get your students thinking outside the box.

Promoting Active Participation

ChatGPT can be used as a virtual discussion partner to make the conversation more interesting and get students to take part. Teachers can host online debates, discussions, and even simulated job interviews with ChatGPT. Not only do students who use ChatGPT receive quick feedback on their contributions, but they are also prompted to provide more thorough explanations of their reasoning. This dynamic of interactivity can significantly improve the educational process.

Promoting Curiosity

ChatGPT's wealth of information is a strength. Students' innate curiosity can be stoked by tapping into this body of information. ChatGPT can give students in-depth responses to their inquiries and connect them to other reading and viewing materials. This not only answers their questions but also encourages them to learn more.

Instant Feedback for Improvement

When you use ChatGPT to help you learn, you can get feedback immediately. When students are having difficulty grasping a concept, they have the option to ask questions and/or be given more information. Real-time communication can help them understand better and keep them interested by quickly addressing their knowledge gaps.

Best ChatGPT Prompts to Get Students Involved

This section is your go-to whether you're looking for creative ways to encourage learning or need help keeping your class engaged. Find solutions to this common problem and give teachers some fun, fresh ideas for getting students involved.

Argument Jumpstarters:

"Give out discussion starters for fifth grade social studies classes to spark conversation."

Collaborative Tasks:

"How can I plan a group exercise to engage and teach first graders?"

Conversational Educating:

"To better engage second graders in geographical learning, please suggest some engaging activities."

Encouragement and Reward"

"Can you provide strategies for encouraging primary school students to finish their work on time?"

Teachers can use these questions to facilitate student-centered learning through dialogue, collaborative projects, and other forms of student-centered instruction. Keeping pupils interested in learning ensures the classroom is a fun place for everyone.

Additional AI Tools for Interactive Classrooms

Brainly

Brainly is an AI-driven digital platform that brings together teachers and students from all around the world to work together on educational projects. It's a Q&A site where students may post homework questions and get answers from their other students and teachers. Brainly makes use of AI-based matching algorithms to provide you with relevant and helpful responses to your questions.

Edpuzzle

Edpuzzle is an AI-driven interactive video platform that uses personalized video lectures to keep students interested and engaged in their education. Edpuzzle lets teachers make their own videos or collect videos from different sources. They can also add interactive features like quizzes and analytics to let teachers see how well their students are learning and progressing. To further encourage interactive learning, the technology includes the opportunity to incorporate in-video comments and notes.

Grammarly

If you're a teacher, you can get some help with your writing and with giving students feedback on theirs by using Grammarly, an AI-based writing aid. Using AI, it evaluates text for typos, grammatical faults, spelling mistakes, and style inconsistencies, then offers instant feedback and corrections. Grammarly also helps with academic writing by spotting plagiarized content, improving vocabulary, and offering other writing resources.

Nearpod

Nearpod is an arena for interactive presentations and group learning that is driven by AI and is meant to keep students interested. It provides a wealth of multimedia tools, such as interactive slides, VR experiences, and formative evaluations. With Nearpod, educators can design engaging, interactive lessons for their students, track their progress in real time, and offer constructive criticism.

Quillbot

Quillbot is an AI-powered writing assistance tool created to help educators and students become better writers. Powered by sophisticated machine learning and natural language processing algorithms, Quillbot may make recommendations, rephrase sentences, and improve grammar and vocabulary. It's like having a personal writing coach right at your fingertips, helping you in polishing your work's readability, organization, and style.

Quizlet

Quizlet is a tool driven by AI that helps teachers make interactive content for their students to study and tests for them. The user-friendly interface of Quizlet allows educators to design unique flashcards, tests, and activities for their classrooms. Quizlet's AI can also adapt to different learning styles. It evaluates how well students are doing on tests and quizzes, and then uses that information to personalize their learning plans. Students can interact with one another through study set sharing and group activities thanks to Quizlet's AI-powered assistance for collaborative learning.

Socrative

With Socrative, teachers can check how much their students know in real time using tests and quizzes, give each student individualized feedback, and encourage group work with activities, projects, and homework. Its many useful functions and features can help educators design valid tests and provide valuable feedback to improve student performance.

Key Takeaways

- Traditional methods struggle to engage students and promote agency in learning.
- Academic success and life skills depend on student participation.
- ChatGPT, part of AI, encourages student innovation, active participation, and inquiry.
- Classrooms can benefit from interactive teaching, AI-generated content, and varied views from ChatGPT.

Chapter 6
Saving Time with AI

A teacher's busy daily life involves spending a lot of their precious time on things that are necessary but don't directly involve teaching. There's a lot on their plates between grading, meeting deadlines, and caring for their children, leaving whatever time is left over to focus on what matters most.

A recent survey sheds light on this. About five hours a week is spent on grading and giving comments to students, another five hours is spent on careful planning and preparation, and the remaining three hours are spent on miscellaneous administrative tasks (Hardison, 2022). Being a teacher requires more than just teaching when you add the hours spent interacting with students outside of school, working with other teachers, talking to parents, and many other things.

Let's consider a real-world scenario. Mr. Parker is a typical educator who likes to do things the old-fashioned way in the classroom. To kick off each day, he must complete a mountain of paperwork, such as lesson plans, student evaluations, and attendance records. Hours are wasted by him in manually calculating grades, keeping track of attendance, and arranging classroom supplies. He frequently finds himself unable to devote sufficient time to classroom instruction and student interaction due to administrative demands.

He's worn out when class starts, and his students can feel the tension in the room. His lectures are always the same, and he never changes the content. There isn't much student engagement, and many students have trouble connecting with the course subject. Mr. Parker doesn't have much time for one-on-one conversations or personalized help, so some of his students feel like they don't have any support.

Teachers' Morale and the Toll of Administrative Work

Independent Schools Victoria (ISV) recently did a study that shows the challenges teachers in Victoria's private schools face. The majority of Victoria's private school teachers are enthusiastic about their work; indeed, many see their profession as a vocation rather than a job, according to the poll. However, the results also show a serious problem that hurts their morale.

The survey found that a shocking 78% of private school teachers in Victoria feel that their morale has suffered due to having to spend too much time on administrative activities (Henebery, 2023). This number shows how much teachers have to do outside of teaching and how this takes their focus away from their primary job, which is to teach and care for their students.

Over three-quarters (78%) of educators say they would prefer a lighter workload if it were divided more evenly between teaching and other responsibilities (Henebery, 2023). This includes paperwork and being responsible for things that often get in the way of their desire to make a change in the lives of their students. Moreover, over half of the educators said they needed help meeting the varying needs of their students, and many of them went looking for it.

The problems don't just happen in the classroom; 47% of teachers say that talking to parents is their least favorite part of the job (Henebery, 2023). Not feeling appreciated or respected at work by others is another thing that can make people unhappy and less likely to stay with their company.

Similar results have been found in studies from a range of school types, such as public and private schools. Like their peers in other fields, those who teach at private schools must contend with the excessive expectations of some parents and a general lack of respect for their knowledge. Taking care of these issues is essential for the health and happiness of teachers and the well-being of the teaching staff as a whole.

How AI Automates and Speeds Up Administrative Duties

Now, let's consider another scenario. Ms. Diane teaches in the same school as Mr. Parker and advocates using AI in the classroom. She streamlines her administrative duties with the help of a suite of AI-driven applications. The first thing she does each day is to use an AI-powered digital attendance system to swiftly update her files. With the help of AI-powered software that grades and delivers immediate feedback on projects, she no longer has to spend hours every week grading.

Without the distraction of administrative duties, Ms. Diane can finally devote more time to what she enjoys most: teaching. She uses AI-generated content to build engaging courses for her students that are tailored to their individual needs. Through the use of AI chatbots to make learning more interactive, her students are fully involved in class discussions and group projects. So much so that she even uses AI chatbots to run virtual discussions and debates.

Her class is full of enthusiastic learners because of it. They work together on tasks while asking questions, discussing different viewpoints, and sharing ideas. Ms. Diane is now better able to devote her time to each of her students, providing them with the kind of individualized attention that will ultimately lead to their growth as people and as students.

Ms. Diane has time outside of the classroom to be involved in extracurricular activities including leading the robotics club and guiding the debate squad. She has the time and resources to continue her education, participate in professional organizations, and learn about cutting-edge methods in the classroom. Her students gain from her boundless energy and the many opportunities she presents them.

Ms. Diane is just one example of how a forward-thinking educator can benefit from AI in the classroom by reducing her administrative burden while simultaneously improving her teaching and the lives of her students.

As is evident with Ms. Dinae, less time spent on paperwork means teachers can have more mental capacity to devote to their primary responsibility: instructing children. Here are a few examples of how AI might significantly improve a teacher's daily routines:

Analysis and Management of Data

Data on students can be easily gathered, organized, and analyzed by AI systems. Teachers can see how each student is doing and adjust their lessons accordingly. By spotting at-risk students early on, this data-driven strategy can boost educational outcomes for everyone.

Content Aggregation

Learning materials can be found and curated with the help of AI. Teachers don't have to spend time looking for materials because it can suggest articles, videos, and other resources that are important to their lessons.

Grading by Computer

Teachers spend a lot of time grading assignments and tests, which is an administrative burden. This can be automated using AI-powered technologies, and all teachers would have to do is examine and approve the final outcome. AI can help teachers pinpoint where their students are having trouble and provide them with specific suggestions to improve.

Help with Communication

AI can help with everyday communication tasks like reminding people of events, setting up discussions between parents and teachers, and responding to frequently asked questions. To put it another way, this means that classroom time, rather than being spent responding to administrative emails, will be used to educate students.

Paperwork for the Administration

Reports, paperwork, and administrative forms can all be created by AI software. AI can help teachers save time and minimize paperwork by automating processes like taking attendance, generating progress reports, and issuing individualized certificates.

Prioritizing Tasks

AI can help teachers organize their work. AI can help teachers prioritize their workload by prioritizing activities based on their significance and the amount of time left until they are due.

Report Making

AI can quickly compile and organize information into professional documents for parents or managers, so teachers don't have to spend as much time handling administrative duties.

Record-keeping and Attendance

Automating attendance tracking using AI streamlines the process and eliminates the potential for human error. It can also handle the administration of student files, ensuring that all relevant data is kept up-to-date and readily available.

AI Tools for Administrative Duties

The availability and popularity of AI-powered solutions for the classroom are on the rise. Teachers can make better use of their time and materials in the classroom by incorporating AI technology. These AI-powered tools won't just make you a better educator; they'll also help your students achieve their full potential in the classroom!

Education CoPilot

Every school should have access to Education CoPilot, a helpful AI tool for educators. Teachers can use this software to make lesson plans, generate PowerPoint, student handouts, reports, writing prompts, and keep account of their students' progress. It also helps teachers construct personalized learning strategies for each student. And what better AI helper could a teacher ask for than this? It's truly remarkable how quickly Education CoPilot can create custom lesson plans, handouts, and other instructional materials tailored to your needs.

There are free and premium versions of Education CoPilot available. While the free version already has a wealth of useful tools, an upgrade to the subscription version is recommended if you need access to more sophisticated tools like AI templates, editing, document long-form handout production, and auto-save.

SlidesAI.io

Quickly and easily generate visually beautiful and interesting presentations for use in the classroom using SlidesAI, a sophisticated AI application. It employs cutting-edge AI technology to automatically produce presentation slides and layouts from text input, freeing you to concentrate on the presentation's content. It also provides suggestions for accompanying visuals based on the presentation's subject matter.

SlidesAI's unique features include its compatibility with Google Workspace and its library of customizable themes and layouts. Because of its zero-dollar price tag, Slides AI is a top pick for schools with limited funds. It also has premium plans starting at USD 10.60 per month that provide access to features like high-resolution presentation export and exclusive themes.

Formative AI

Formative AI is an AI application designed to help educators in evaluating student work. It immediately responds to student work, highlighting both strengths and deficiencies so that instructors can better tailor their lessons to each individual student. Formative AI saves teachers time by doing the grading for them and giving them information about how their students are doing that they can use to plan better lessons in the future.

Multiple-choice, free-form, true/false, and image-based questions are just a few of the assessment types that can be used. In this approach, educators have the option of starting from scratch or using the available templates to design classroom evaluations quickly and easily.

Features that set Formative AI apart from other educational resources include its capacity to tailor instruction to each individual student. It employs AI-based algorithms to evaluate student work and offer constructive criticism. This allows for more personalized instruction and intervention for each learner. The best part? You can use it for free.

Gradescope

Gradescope is an AI-powered grading and evaluation application recently gaining popularity among teachers. It's meant to make grading papers, assignments, and tests easier and faster. The best thing is that Gradescope can handle grading in various disciplines and academic levels, including the sciences and the humanities.

Gradescope's unique features include an embedded plagiarism checker that allows educators to check for plagiarized content without leaving the platform. Gradescope also offers in-depth analytics for educators to use in pinpointing problem areas. It has both free and premium versions available. In the premium edition, you can create your own rubrics, connect with other apps, and work together with your team.

PowerPoint Speaker Coach

PowerPoint Speaker Coach is designed to do just what its name implies: assist lecturers in giving lively and informative presentations to their students. The software evaluates the speaker's tempo, pitch, and intensity during a PowerPoint presentation and then recommends enhancement.

If you're a teacher looking to energize your classroom presentations with PowerPoint Speaker Coach, you've found the right software. Teachers can improve students' attention and participation by adjusting their delivery. The resource is especially helpful for first-year educators or experienced teachers looking for a refresher course in presentation skills.

Use the "Slide Show" menu > "Rehearse with Coach" option in the PowerPoint web app to access the Speaker Coach.

PowerPoint Speaker Coach generates a rehearsal report with essential data including tempo, filler word usage, sensitivity phrase usage, overall time, and areas for development. It has both a free and a premium version available. Additional features, such as in-depth analysis and comments, are available in the premium version.

Key Takeaways

- Teachers' capacity to teach is sometimes compromised by the time they spend on paperwork and other administrative duties.
- Many educators say they'd be happier if they could devote more time to really teaching and making an influence on their pupils.
- By automating routine administrative work, AI solutions allow educators to focus more on student learning.

Chapter 7

Professional Development in the AI Era

I have no special talent. I am only passionately curious. –Albert Einstein

In the era of AI, this chapter stands as a monument to the ever-changing nature of the teaching profession and a beacon to all educators and teachers. The words of Albert Einstein ring true as you set out on a journey that will require your insatiable curiosity and a set of skills befitting the age of AI. Your dedication to lifelong learning as an educator is more important than ever. You shape the minds and hearts of tomorrow's leaders.

Your position as an educator takes on new significance in a world where the pace of technological advancement accelerates daily, and AI impacts the future of learning. This section will help you see AI not as an enemy but as a potential ally in the quest to improve the educational system. It will provide you with the knowledge and skills you need to confidently adapt to the AI age and take the helm of your organization.

The rise of AI isn't a threat to the teaching profession; rather, it's a chance to innovate in the classroom, inspire students in new ways, and pave the road to a limitless educational future. Whether you're an experienced teacher or just starting out, the information in this chapter can help you in your quest to make education more meaningful for your students.

Education in the age of AI is not a fixed pursuit; rather, it is fluid, responsive, and motivated by your insatiable desire to know. This chapter is meant to provide you with the tools you need to adapt to the rapidly developing field of education.

The Significance of Continuous Learning as an Educator

In a world where everything is constantly changing, it is more important than ever to keep learning throughout your life. The workplace has changed dramatically as a result of technological developments and the accessibility of worldwide connections. A commitment to lifelong learning is essential for success in today's highly competitive job market.

The time and effort put into one's own development paves the way for a more fulfilling and fruitful professional life and can even facilitate a change in the field. Moreover, lifelong education has been connected to improved spirits, greater contentment on the job, and a more robust perception of one's own value.

So, what exactly is lifelong education? "Upskilling" means getting new skills and information all the time, which is what continuous learning means. People develop on both a personal and professional level as a result of this effort, expanding their horizons and realizing their full potential. Another term you might hear is "lifelong learning," which is similar but typically refers to individual growth in areas unrelated to career.

Learning never stops and lasts a lifetime. It can take several shapes to fit different people's tastes. Taking evening classes at a nearby institution, reading bite-sized educational content, or taking part in online courses are just a few of the many options for expanding knowledge and moving beyond one's current position.

How Can Continuous Education Help You?

Among the many upsides to lifelong education are:

- **Growing in self-assurance.** You'll feel more confident in taking on professional challenges or exploring new chances when you know you've improved your skill set.
- **Professional growth.** Acquiring new abilities can help you advance in your current position or perhaps open doors to new opportunities. If you're between employment, or already employed, showing that you're dedicated to learning new skills will make you stand out to potential employers and increase your value to your present organization.
- **Acquiring new skills and credentials or refreshing your existing ones.** Continuous learning might help you maintain your momentum and knowledge base if your employment requires you to get or renew specific certifications or qualifications on a regular basis.
- **Taking a new look at things.** Your beliefs and values may shift as you acquire new knowledge. If you're committed to lifelong learning, you'll get a deeper comprehension of potential challenges and the ability to identify and implement solutions you might not have considered previously.
- **Productivity increases.** Increased output is a win-win for businesses and their employees when workers report higher levels of personal satisfaction. This may affect both employee satisfaction and the company's ability to retain its best workers.
- **Motivational speech.** If you set an example for people around you by demonstrating the value of education, they may be encouraged to pursue their own educational goals. Ultimately, this could make your workplace better.

Options for Continuous Education

There are many ways for educators to improve their skills, such as through free online tools, colleges and universities, conferences, and professional development. Educators can use these channels to hone their craft, expand their horizons, and keep abreast of the latest findings in the field.

Conferences

Educators who attend various conferences can improve their teaching and grading practices in the classroom. These can range from small, intimate gatherings to larger, more formal meetings lasting several days.

Higher Education

Higher education, like university or college classes, allows educators to make their learning fit with the certifications they already have or to learn about new things. It's a great opportunity to get out of your comfort zone and learn about new things, plus it can help you get a degree or certification.

Keep It In-house

Internal seminars and informal gatherings with colleagues are two examples of professional development activities. They can cover things like standards-based grading, group learning, and more, and they can be changed to fit each person's needs. Institutional and regional budgets frequently fund continual education for teachers and administrators.

Never-ending education provides teachers with better classroom management skills, allowing for more quality time with their students. It encourages critical thinking, which is beneficial since it helps cultivate an atmosphere where interest and inquiry flourish. Additionally, ongoing learning is a vital part of professional development, which can reignite teachers' enthusiasm and, in the end, make the learning experience better for their students.

Learn More with ChatGPT and Beyond

The benefits of ChatGPT go far beyond its use in the classroom. Its extensive expertise and natural conversational skills allow it to give readers helpful advice and suggestions that are specific to their needs. ChatGPT can provide advice, recommend resources, and even produce practice activities for any effort, be it learning a new language, starting a creative project, or diving into a new technical skill. This tool is a great way to meet like-minded people and learn about new techniques and approaches to improving yourself.

Additionally, it can help you establish individual learning objectives and monitor your development. It can keep you motivated to continue your education by providing timely feedback, reminders, and words of praise. ChatGPT may be a helpful companion for anyone learning something new, whether that's a musical instrument, a new cuisine, or the world of coding. It encourages people to be curious and keep learning in ways that go beyond the classroom. You can use this tool to help them develop their interests, unearth latent skills, and set off on enriching paths to self-improvement.

The benefits of using ChatGPT extend far beyond the classroom, and it could have a major impact on your professional and personal life. Here's a deep dive into the ways in which ChatGPT could help you:

Partner in Solving Problems

When working to solve an issue, ChatGPT might be a helpful resource. It can help you deal with issues in your personal life, at work, or in making important choices. ChatGPT helps you quickly tackle challenges by assessing problems, providing alternative viewpoints, and suggesting solutions.

Proper Time-keeping

Successful people are good at managing their time. ChatGPT can offer advice, methods, and individualized plans to help you maximize your productivity. ChatGPT is a helpful time management counselor that can be used to optimize calendars, create priorities, and discover productivity hacks.

Constant Education

The classroom is just one part of a lifetime of education. Based on your hobbies and professional aspirations, ChatGPT can suggest a variety of books, courses, and resources. ChatGPT can be your own learning guide, whether you're trying to keep up with a dynamic field or learn something completely new.

Competence in Language and Speech

In both personal and professional contexts, the ability to communicate clearly and effectively is essential. You can use ChatGPT to learn new words, get advice on your work, and get pointers on how to better express yourself verbally and in writing. This can help you communicate more clearly, persuasively, and assuredly in a variety of settings.

Career Growth

ChatGPT can also be used as a professional counselor. It can help you figure out what you want to do with your life, find out about job openings, and even make your resume or cover letter stand out. If you're getting ready for an interview, ChatGPT can help by providing sample questions and suggestions for effective responses.

Coping with Stress

Modern life has a number of challenges, and one of them is stress. Tips on how to relax, how to be more aware, and other strategies for dealing with stress are all within the scope of ChatGPT. ChatGPT can help you feel better emotionally by teaching you healthy ways to deal with stress.

Preparation and Goal Setting

Whether you're looking to improve your personal life or advance your career, ChatGPT can help you define your goals, develop a plan of action, and maintain your enthusiasm. It can keep tabs on your development and send you timely reminders to keep you on track.

How ChatGPT Can Improve Personal and Professional Life

These real-world examples show how ChatGPT may be helpful in a variety of settings, from the personal to the professional, providing support, motivation, and direction in a wide range of endeavors. The following are some concrete situations where individuals have benefited from using ChatGPT in their daily lives:

- Sarah, a marketer, utilizes ChatGPT to come up with interesting topics for blog posts and material for her social media accounts. She gives ChatGPT a quick summary of her intended readers and the topic at hand, and it generates original content ideas that save her time and improve the quality of her writing.
- Alex is studying a foreign language in preparation for an upcoming business trip abroad. He practices speaking the language and gets instant feedback from ChatGPT. As a result, his confidence soars, and he gains language proficiency.
- Technical writer John relies on ChatGPT for peer review and editing of his work. When it comes to writing professionally, he relies heavily on ChatGPT's feedback on grammar, punctuation, and style.
- Emily is a teacher who uses ChatGPT to generate ideas for new and exciting ways to teach and learn in her classroom. Her students find her lessons more interesting, thanks to the new insights they gain from ChatGPT.
- Student Michael requires assistance with writing a research report. By entering his topic of study and research queries, ChatGPT generates summaries, key ideas, and possible sources, saving him a great deal of time.

- Lisa utilizes ChatGPT as a personal coach to work on improving herself. She has talks using ChatGPT in which she shares her goals and struggles. ChatGPT provides guidance, inspiration, and individualized plans of action to help her succeed.
- Job-seeker Brian needs help with his resume. He relies on ChatGPT to help him develop an impressive application package. ChatGPT recommends persuasive language and revises his applications based on the job postings he is applying to.
- Donna, a would-be business owner, uses ChatGPT as a sounding board for her ideas about potential new ventures. To help her perfect her ideas, ChatGPT offers insightful criticism and information about the market.

Prompts for Personal and Professional Development

Here are a few prompts to help you in your professional endeavors and also help you grow as a person:

Self-Reflection

"Help me figure out what my core values are as a teacher and how they fit with my job."

Goal Setting

"Help me turn my dreams of becoming a teacher into SMART goals that I can actually reach."

Time Management

"Help me learn how to better organize my time so that I may devote more of my energy to educating my students."

Self-Care

"Give me some ideas for how I may take care of my health, mind, and spirit while still pursuing a career in education."

Appreciation

"Help me cultivate an attitude of gratitude by highlighting the bright spots in my educational experience."

Personalized Professional Development

"Give me specific advice and suggestions on how to improve my teaching and reach my professional goals."

Creative Lesson Design

"Give ideas and tools for making interesting lesson plans that work for all kinds of learning styles."

Fusion of Technologies

"Give some ideas on how to use technology to get students more involved and help them learn better."

Personal and Professional Resources from Other AI Tools

Vital—A Companion for Mindfulness

- Formerly know as Ogimi AI, Vital is a helpful tool for cultivating awareness through tailored meditation sessions, game-like challenges, and friendly competition.
- Reduced stress, enhanced concentration, greater emotional stability, and higher-quality sleep are just some of the advantages.
- There's a free version with some restrictions and a paid one with additional customization options.

Habit Driven—Habit Cultivation App

- Habit Driven employs AI to help people form good routines and accomplish their objectives.

- Provides instant analysis, in-depth articles, and hassle-free routine tracking.
- Connects to your fitness and banking apps.
- The basic version is free, while a paid premium edition is available for more features and deeper analytics.

Personal AI—Digital Personal Assistant

- Users can make their own digital personal helper with Personal AI, which helps them be more productive and remember things.
- Information collection, management, and retrieval are all simplified by a knowledge engine that may be tailored by AI.
- There is a free, basic version with fewer options and the ability to upgrade to a paid plan with more features and flexibility.

TalkPal AI—Learn Languages with ChatGPT Technology

- Using ChatGPT technology, TalkPal AI provides one-on-one language instruction.
- Improves one's abilities in hearing, talking, reading, and writing.
- Features an adaptive voice function and listening exercises that mimic real life.
- You can try it out for free, and you can subscribe to get access to more tools and language options.

NetworkAI—AI-Powered Networking Tool

- Developed by WonsultingAI, NetworkAI automatically sends out personalized LinkedIn introduction messages, rapidly expanding professional networks.
- Provides tools for keeping track of networking results, prioritizing connections, and reaching out to key influencers.
- Multiple subscription tiers offer varied token quantities.

Key Takeaways

- In an AI-driven school system, continuous learning will be critical for educators.
- AI can help you come up with new ways to teach.
- ChatGPT can help you grow personally and professionally in many ways.

Chapter 8
Ensuring Data Privacy and Security

With all of these great technological advances we've discussed so far, there is one big worry: how AI will affect privacy and security. You may be wondering what protections are in place to keep personal information safe in this new age of education. Since AI can handle huge amounts of data, protecting the privacy and safety of students, teachers, and institutions becomes highly important.

Nowadays, data is worth a lot, so keeping it safe is not only the law but the right thing to do. Now, let's look into the complicated link between AI and keeping private data safe in the schooling field. My top priority is to provide you with the information you need to tackle this challenging environment confidently. Come with me as I look into essential strategies for protecting privacy and security.

Defining Data Privacy in the AI Era

When trying to balance privacy and AI, the first problem is figuring out what the terms mean. Each country and U.S. state has passed its own data protection law since the General Data Protection Regulation (GDPR) went into effect, with a slightly different definition of what personal data is.

Personal data, according to the GDPR, is any information about an identified or identifiable natural person ("Data Subject"). It includes real-world data such as names, addresses, Social Security numbers, and more.

Since its inception in 2002, the California Consumer Privacy Act (CCPA) has expanded its original scope to include things like biometric data, internet activity records, geolocation, and others (State of California Department of Justice, 2023). As of January 1, 2023, the California Privacy Rights Act (CPRA) added new types of "sensitive data," such as Social Security numbers and genetic data, that need extra protections on top of the protections for other personal information (Gopalasamy, 2022). Because of this, any organization that wants to follow and stay in line with present and potential data privacy rules must first ask themselves, "What types of data are we protecting?"

Neither the General Data Protection Regulation nor the California Consumer Privacy Act mention AI by name. Still, they address the broader idea of "automated individual decision-making," which now incorporates AI and machine learning. Article 22 of the GDPR, for instance, specifies that individuals have the right to not be subjected to a decision based purely on automated processing, such as profiling, when such a decision will have a significant or legally binding impact on the individual (Intersoft Consulting, n.d.). A number of state and federal rules are also being worked on to deal with AI and privacy directly.

Challenges in AI-Driven Data Collection

Collecting customer data is relatively straightforward when it is provided knowingly, such as during a purchase. In such cases, individuals provide their full name, street address, and credit card information and may have legal protections to keep this data safe. However, certain AI implementations, like the use of AI-powered security cameras to collect data, add complexity to the situation. While these cameras can recognize faces and link them to individuals, those whose data is collected may not be aware of it or understand how it will be used. This makes it challenging to comply with regulations like the GDPR and advocate for consumer rights such as the right to be informed, the right to be forgotten, or the right to limit data processing.

There is also growing concern about the potential for accidental biases in AI and data, which can lead to unfair results based on private information. Since AI systems are trained using data generated by humans, these biases can become embedded in the system. A notable example of this is when Amazon stopped using a hiring program that was biased against women. This means that companies and organizations that use AI to analyze customer data must now comply with data privacy regulations and take measures to safeguard their customers' trust.

A Blueprint for an AI Bill of Rights

The White House's publication of a "Blueprint for an AI Bill of Rights" represents a noteworthy government initiative in this area (The White House, 2022). In situations where automated systems pose a serious threat to human rights, freedoms, or access to essential services, this plan seeks to offer some direction. It has two basic tenets: explainability (clarifying how something is done) and transparency (describing the actions being taken).

More so, four broad "expectations" are laid forth for automated systems in the Data Privacy part of the blueprint.

1. Enable privacy protections by default in systems.
2. Stop unregulated surveillance that could harm the public.
3. Make it easy for people to give their consent, see their data, and stay in charge.
4. Prove that you care about users' right to privacy and control over their data.

In any case, the fact that the United States government is even considering issues of AI and personal privacy and is drafting a non-binding paper to that effect is noteworthy.

Customer Sentiment and AI

Consumer sentiment is a powerful argument for businesses to balance AI deployment with privacy safeguards. Over and over again, consumer trust in a company is found to be directly proportional to how responsibly that organization handles its customers' personal information. The advent of AI has only increased the significance of this link.

Even while most Americans don't know much about the specifics of AI, they do know that there could be problems with their personal information if they use it. This was demonstrated by a recent survey performed by Cisco, which found that 60% of consumers are worried about how AI would use their personal data. Also, 65% of those who answered said they had lost trust in certain organizations because they used AI technology (Cisco, 2023).

Data and Privacy Security in Educational Institutions

After the pandemic, concerns around data security, privacy, and protection in schools have gotten a lot of attention. The recent closing of two Skinners' Kent schools in Tunbridge Wells as a result of data breaches is a stark warning of how important it is to prioritize data protection and security. According to the Cyber Security Leaks Survey, 36% of elementary schools and 58% of secondary schools have reported leaks or cyberattacks (Thompson, 2021).

This is an alarming pattern. These numbers are a little lower than they were last year, but leave questions as to how well tracking and reporting are working, especially since the COVID-19 pandemic forced people to switch to remote learning.

With the switch to online learning came both pros and cons. It was a lifesaver for keeping education going, but it also showed where weaknesses were. Hackers were able to easily get to personal data, leaving students open to a number of risks. A lot of institutions might not have had the protection they thought they did.

One big challenge that came up during the global pandemic was whether or not school staff were properly trained for online delivery. As educators rushed to embrace online education, many safety measures were left unchecked. Personal information about students and their families was open to cyberattacks because of this lack of planning. According to the Cyber Security Breaches Survey, just a third of elementary schools and four out of ten high schools have conducted cybersecurity training and awareness activities in the recent year (Department for Science, Innovation and Technology, 2023).

A big hole in data protection has been found because digital platforms for education were quickly adopted without giving their safety or security measures much thought. It is extremely important to look at platform usage and decision-making with more critical eyes.

Personal information must be safeguarded at all costs. This data could include private things like bank account numbers, addresses, and passwords that could be used against people if they get hacked. Making sure that users are safe from internet threats is very important for educational platforms.

Cyberattacks have happened to even colleges, and data has been held for ransom. This shows how important strong online security steps are. Staff should get ongoing training to keep them up to date on new threats and problems. The best way for educational organizations to protect data and privacy as technology changes is to stay informed and up-to-date.

Issues with Data Privacy in AI-Powered Classrooms

The use of AI in the classroom has unquestionably improved teaching and learning, streamlined administrative processes, and provided students with more individualized content. However, it also raises a number of data privacy risks that teachers must be alert of in order to protect their student data and their own personal information.

Accessibility

All students, especially those with special needs, should have equal access to AI learning resources. It is morally and legally required that AI systems meet accessibility requirements.

Safeguarding Student Data

One of the biggest worries about using AI in education is that a lot of information about each student, like personal details, academic success, and behavior patterns, is collected and processed. Keeping this information safe from people who shouldn't have access to it and following data security laws like the Family Educational Rights and Privacy Act (FERPA) are highly recommended.

Ethical Data Mining

Teachers should use caution when implementing recommendations and insights generated by AI. The misuse of AI-generated data can result in prejudice and injury, such as when used to assign students to classes based on preconceived notions.

Data Safety

Strong security measures are required to shield AI systems in academic institutions from hacking and data breaches. These hacks can make private school data public, hurt trust, and even get people in trouble with the law.

Consent and Openness

It is the responsibility of educators to ensure that AI algorithms are open and transparent and to gain the appropriate permission from pupils, their parents, or guardians before collecting and using their personal information.

Targeting and Profiling

An increasing issue is the potential for compiling comprehensive profiles of pupils for the sake of targeted advertising or some other reason. Preventing students from being subjected to unsolicited advertising or profiling is crucial.

Data Retention Guidelines

If you want to lessen the blow of a data breach, you need to define data retention terms and stick to them.

International Data Exchange

Educators need to think about the ramifications of foreign data privacy rules and regulations if they implement AI technologies that require the movement of data across borders.

Model Quality in AI

For AI models to be used in education, they must be of high quality and fair. Students can be treated unfairly and discriminated against by AI models that are biased.

Rights to Data

It can be difficult to sort out who owns the information that AI systems produce or collect in classroom settings. It is of the utmost importance to set up explicit ownership rights.

If schools and teachers want to use AI to help students learn, they need to address these issues right away. To do this, we need to set up a strong data privacy framework, keep up with data protection rules, and encourage people to use AI responsibly. In this way, teachers can create a safe and moral AI-powered learning space that is good for both pupils and staff.

Data and Privacy Protection Strategies

There is a growing importance on protecting students' personal information as teachers integrate AI into their lesson plans and administrative processes. It is not only a legal necessity but also an ethical obligation to put measures in place to protect sensitive information. You can use the following advice and methods to protect their data when working with AI:

Data Encryption: To keep data safe, both while it's being sent and while it's being stored, use encryption methods. Data encryption makes it more difficult for hackers to access sensitive information.

How to: Make sure your online learning tools use safe ways to communicate, like HTTPS. Files stored on servers should be encrypted to protect data at rest. Make use of features like Windows' BitLocker and macOS' FileVault.

Regular Security Checks: To find weak spots in your AI data and systems stores, do regular security checks. Rapidly addressing any problems that may arise.

How to: Perform frequent audits by either employing automated vulnerability scanning technologies or employing a third-party security agency. Use a vulnerability scanner like Nessus once every three months.

Access Controls: Make sure that only people who are allowed to see private data can find it by putting strict access controls in place. Incorporate role-based access controls.

How to: Make your Learning Management System (LMS) safer by adding role-based access controls. Teachers should be given access to student information but should be prevented from making any changes.

Minimize Data: Reduce the amount of data collected and stored to the bare minimum required for instructional reasons. Keeping records to a minimum reduces the potential damage from a hack.

How-to: Limit yourself to the very minimum while asking for information from students. If you need a mailing address for a survey or census, but not a street address, ask for the zip code.

Data Anonymization: Eliminate personally identifying information (PII) without compromising the data's use in AI.

How to: Hack tools that make data anonymous to eliminate personally identifiable information (PII). The Anonymizer program can remove personal information such as names and addresses before data is shared with researchers, for instance.

Consent and Transparency: Make sure that parents, students, or guardians give clear and informed consent before you store and use their data. Explain in detail how you intend to use the information.

How to: Make the need for data collecting crystal clear to students and parents throughout orientation. Provide a pop-up box describing data usage and requesting authorization from students, for example, when they register.

Educational Privacy Policies: Make and share clear privacy policies that explain how data is protected and what people's rights are.

How to: Put your institution's privacy statement online. Make sure that information on student rights and data security procedures is included. Provide a contact number or email for questions.

Information Portability: Make sure that parents, students, or workers can easily access their information and move it around as needed. Regulations for data sharing must be followed.

How to: Create a student portal so they can see and download their school information. Provide standardized export options, such as PDF and CSV, at parents' request.

Data Retention Policies: Make rules about how long data will be kept and when it will be safely removed, and make sure they are followed.

How to: Draft a policy that mandates student files to be kept for five years following graduation, after which they shall be destroyed safely. Automate this procedure with the help of data management tools.

Staff Training: Teach teachers, managers, and support staff the best ways to keep data safe. Make sure they understand what is expected of them and the potential consequences.

How to: Teach your staff about data safety once a year. Build interactive modules and tests for them to take online to test their knowledge of their duties.

Patching and Updates: Protect AI software, apps, and systems from known vulnerabilities by updating security patches regularly.

How to: Make sure that the latest versions of your LMS and AI tools are always installed. You should set your program to automatically update or establish a regular update routine.

Third-Party Vendors: If you use AI solutions from a third party, get to know how they handle data safety and ensure they follow the law.

How to: Learn about the company's data protection policies before buying an AI-powered learning platform. Inquire about their privacy and security measures and determine how well they fit the needs of your organization.

Security Awareness Programs: Teach your students why data privacy and cybersecurity are essential. Encourage a mindset of accountability in data management.

How to: Set up sessions for students to learn about cybersecurity. Explain what phishing emails are and how to spot them. Encourage them to report questionable behavior by offering them incentives.

Prepare an Incident Reaction Plan: It should spell out what to do in the event of a data breach. This plan should be clear and easy to follow. Maintain regular practice and hone your approach.

How to: Draft a policy detailing what should be done in the event of a data breach. Staff should go through a mock breach simulation to practice their response.

Ethical AI: Promote accountable AI use in your organization. Avoid using AI in ways that violate students' privacy or cause them to be treated unfairly.

How to: provide instructions for educators on how to implement AI-based assessment and grading safely. Try substituting pseudonyms for actual names.

Compliance with the Law: Ensure you know about and follow all data protection rules in your area, like FERPA, GDPR, or CCPA.

How to: Look over the data security laws that apply to your institution regularly. For the CCPA, for instance, see that you are always up to date.

Regular Backups: Make sure you back up your data often so you don't lose it in case of an accident or hacking.

How to: Make sure that school records are backed up automatically. If you need extra insurance, use a cloud service like Google Drive or Dropbox to back up your data.

Privacy by Design: Make sure that privacy is thought about from the start when developing and using AI systems by following the privacy rules by design.

How to: Incorporate privacy officers or specialists into the development of cutting-edge AI software. They may make sure privacy is taken into account from the beginning of the design process.

Educators may take advantage of AI's promise in the classroom while protecting students' and employees' personal information by using the aforementioned measures. Data and privacy protection is not only the right thing to do but also an essential part of creating a safe and ethical learning environment for everyone involved.

Key Takeaways

- In AI-driven classrooms, protecting student data from hackers is of critical importance.
- Students' right to privacy and the security of their personal information depends on the responsible gathering and use of data.
- To ensure confidence and security in AI applications, educational institutions must promote a culture of privacy, compliance, and ethical data handling.

Chapter 9
Preparing for the Future

Imagine a room full of bright young brains, each one intently interacting with their own AI instructor. The AI instructors are well-versed and patient, and they tailor their lessons to the specific needs of each student in real-time to guarantee they learn everything they need to. This is unlike any other classroom experience because it is an ever-changing relationship between human curiosity and AI. Naturally, we as teachers, parents, and students want to know: how do we factor into this dynamic equation?

In this final section, we set out to discover the potential of AI in the field of education. This chapter gives a holistic picture of the possible future and the concrete actions needed to adjust to the difficulties and new possibilities it brings.

Learn how to explore AI's potential in the classroom, adjust to its inevitable changes, and reap its benefits. This chapter will show you how to open your classroom door to the future and change it into a place where all students can learn and grow.

What Does the Future Hold for AI in Education?

The use of AI in classrooms is expected to skyrocket in the coming year, according to the predictions we discussed. The more AI is used in the classroom, the more intelligent it will become; hence, the possibilities are almost unlimited; yet, I may make the following predictions:

Increasingly Individualized

Students' use of AI-powered learning tools will evolve as they gain expertise in data analysis. This will allow teachers to tailor their lessons to each individual student.

The Realms of VR

Virtual reality (VR) software is expected to become increasingly employed in classrooms to provide students with authentic experiences across a variety of disciplines. Virtual reality (VR) could be used to conduct experiments in the classroom, making them more sophisticated and secure than ever before, as one example.

Student Preparation for the Digital Workplace

There will be a continuing emphasis on teaching students about AI because of its rapidly expanding practical application in the workplace. Students are being prepared for a future when humans and robots work together through the widespread teaching of coding, which introduces them to the concept of giving instructions to a robot (or a program).

Both Sides to AI Emergence

Just like any game-changing invention, the entrance of AI into the education market results in a spectrum of both positive and negative repercussions.

The Upsides of AI in Education

Personalized Learning Priority. One of the most significant advantages of AI in education is the rise of personalized learning, which has been shown to increase student motivation and engagement.

AI systems track pupils' development, identify their areas of weakness, and provide individualized guidance and support. Academic success is better with customized learning, which lets students study at their own pace.

Well-Organized Data. Thanks to AI's ability to categorize data, students may quickly and easily compile information from a wide range of sources. Educational platforms driven by AI can better organize and present data, making it easier for students to access the information they need and improving the quality of their educational experiences.

For instance,

- In business, having well-organized client information is essential for launching effective marketing efforts and providing individualized service.
- Having all of a teacher's resources in one place is a huge time saver and leads to better learning results.
- In your daily life, planning your days and tasks ahead of time makes you more productive and less stressed.

In the grand scheme of things, information organization allows people and businesses to function better and attain their goals quickly.

Helping Students with Disabilities Become Independent. When it comes to accommodating students with varying learning styles, AI can't be topped. Using AI, we can create lessons that adapt to each student's unique learning style and speed, giving them the benefit of individualized instruction.

Improved Academic Standards and Quality in Schools. The use of AI in the classroom is a modern way to pique students' interest in learning.

The use of AI allows for the dynamic modification of course content, the provision of quick feedback, and the evaluation of student engagement beyond that which is possible in traditional educational institutions.

Better Educational Environment. Virtual and augmented reality (VR/AR) are two examples of how AI is enabling more interactive and immersive learning environments. Participating in simulated or real-world settings, under supervision, can help students learn and retain information more effectively. Biology students, for instance, may use a virtual lab to investigate the inner workings of a cell or observe photosynthesis, making the subject more interesting and remembered.

Accessibility. AI technology is a great equalizer since it helps people of all backgrounds and abilities to participate equally in society. Learning tools driven by AI make education available to all students, regardless of their socioeconomic status or geography. One example is the use of AI to power language learning apps, which allow students to study a new language independently at their own speed.

Cost Savings. AI also has the added bonus of helping make education more cost-effective. Automation of labor-intensive processes and the ability to tailor lessons to each individual student are two ways in which technology is helping to bring down the price of a college education. The time and money spent on private tutoring and classroom teachers could be reduced if this were to happen.

The Downsides of AI in the Education

Loss of Employment. The possible reduction of teaching jobs due to AI implementation is a cause for concern. Tools driven by AI can take over crucial parts of a teacher's job, such as grading and giving feedback. Perhaps as a result of this, fewer teaching positions will be available.

The Constraints of Emotional Intelligence. Many people struggle to learn and study because they lack emotional intelligence. Teachers give more than just information, thus AI technology should only replace them in part. Human-AI interaction and personal relationships are still in their early stages, which is why human teachers are still so important to the learning process.

Bias and Inequality. Inequality and prejudice could be the result of biased AI algorithms. For instance, certain students may be unfairly disadvantaged in the admissions process due to the use of AI because of their socioeconomic status or family background. Similar to how certain people may be prejudiced against certain types of answers or writing styles, AI-based grading algorithms may also be biased.

Safety and Confidentiality. Students' actions, academic progress, and personal details are just some of the data collected by AI-powered learning systems. If this information is leaked, pupils' safety and privacy may be at risk from cyberattacks and data breaches. Unauthorized usage of AI systems poses major security risks that have real-world consequences for students.

Technological Dependence. AI-powered learning tools necessitate the utilization of current technology such as computers, cell phones, and the Internet. As a result, people may become less able to think critically and creatively on their own and become more reliant on technology.

Difficulties in Maintenance. Maintenance is one of the challenges of using AI in schooling. Authorities must keep a tight eye on AI systems since they are based on a finite corpus of information and can cause unexpected outcomes if they are overworked. It is possible that different AI machines will not be able to communicate with one another because they use different languages.

How AI Will Change Teaching as It Gets More Accessible

It will be different for teachers in the future as AI becomes easier to use in schools. Let your mind wander to a future classroom where AI is fully integrated into the teaching and learning process:

The classroom is a lively and engaging environment thanks to the smart devices at each student's desk and the enormous interactive displays on the walls. Each student has their own laptop or tablet, and the classroom is set up for collaborative learning. Intelligent system-powered tools are smoothly integrated into the educational setting.

The role of the teacher has shifted from imparting information to that of a guide or facilitator. Rather than staying put at a desk, they circulate the classroom talking to individuals and small groups. Providing one-on-one instruction and coaching is a top priority for them. They can spend more time developing personal and academic rapport with their students.

AI algorithms evaluate the learning preferences, development, and strengths and weaknesses of each student. This information is used by AI-driven systems to design unique lessons and provide suggestions. Teachers can personalize these plans to better assist each individual.

Students can get immediate help from virtual tutors driven by AI. They help students understand difficult subjects by responding to inquiries, providing explanations, and even making interactive simulations. Students can learn whenever and wherever they like with the help of these AI instructors.

In-depth data dashboards provide teachers with information on student progress. They're able to spot students who are failing early on and provide them with individualized help. Using this data-driven method, we can work to prevent students from falling behind.

Students are actively working together in this classroom. AI makes it easier for students to work together on projects and learn from each other, improving their interpersonal and collaborative abilities. Teachers facilitate productive student collaboration.

Teachers use AI tools to create resources that are interesting and useful. Content can be dynamically revised in response to input from students and new developments in the field of education.

As AI takes over more and more mundane duties, teachers can devote more time to developing students' interpersonal and intrapersonal skills. They help open up conversations about analytical thinking, problem-solving, and originality.

Teachers now include discussions of AI ethics, AI critique, and digital citizenship training in their lesson plans. Students benefit from their insight into the ramifications and biases of AI systems.

The use of AI in education allows for more adaptable models like blended and online learning. In this way, students from all over the world, in all time zones, can receive the same high-quality education from the same dedicated teachers. Teachers exemplify the value of a never-ending quest for knowledge and the capacity to roll with the punches of a world where technology is constantly improving.

Teachers play a central role in this AI-enhanced classroom by providing guidance, encouragement, and inspiration to students, while AI handles the mundane responsibilities of delivering and evaluating course material. In the future, humans and machines will work together in tandem to make learning more engaging and unique for each individual.

Adapting to a Classroom Infused with AI

As AI rapidly changes education, educators need to make sure they are ready for the future. To stay up-to-date on AI, take workshops and online classes throughout your life. Work with AI to make training methods more effective and find areas where students are falling behind. Change your lessons to include AI-driven material that is still useful.

Data literacy is important because it lets you look at student data that AI gives you. Offer coding, robots, and AI classes to help students learn digital skills that will be useful in a job market driven by AI. To deal with changes in schooling, build resilience and the ability to adapt.

Connect with other people in educational groups and share how you plan to use AI. Learn about the ethical issues that come up with AI and fight for data privacy and fair methods. Focus on the students and their well-being, and make sure they have a unique learning experience.

Change the way things are done by becoming a supporter of AI integration and an innovator in education. Because AI is now a part of the world, teachers can make learning experiences that are truly changing, making sure that their lessons stay innovative and useful as the field of education evolves.

Key Takeaways

- Teachers' role in helping students build social and emotional skills may be aided by AI, but it won't replace them.
- Learning still requires human-AI interaction and the use of emotional intelligence.
- AI has the potential to revolutionize education by fostering flexibility, individualization, and teamwork.
- Teachers in a classroom with AI emphasize the importance of interpersonal skills, ethics, and flexibility.

Your Review: Paving the Way in AI Education

You've navigated the transformative landscape of AI in education, uncovering the many ways it can revolutionize both teaching and learning.

Just as AI like Siri and Alexa assist us in ways once deemed impossible, your insights can now help guide others in the ever-evolving world of AI education.

By sharing your honest review of "Teaching with AI" on Amazon, you guide other educators toward this innovative approach. Your insights can help pave the way for a more engaged, interactive classroom experience.

Your feedback is more than just words; it's a powerful tool in reshaping the future of education. It supports the shift towards active student participation, where learning is not just about absorbing information but about being deeply engaged and motivated.

Please scan the QR code below to leave a review.

Thank you for being a part of this journey. Your review helps keep the momentum of change in education, ensuring that our classrooms remain vibrant, engaging, and effective for the 21st-century learner.

ModernMind Publications

Conclusion: Embracing the Future with AI

As we wrap up our exploration of AI in education, it's worth pausing to consider the incredible possibilities that lie ahead. In this book, we've covered a wide range of topics related to AI in the classroom with the goal of preparing today's teachers for tomorrow's dynamic learning environments. We've seen how AI can help students learn more, save time, and make the complicated process of merging in education easier.

For us, the journey into the unknown started with a dream, with an overview of the opportunities presented by AI. We progressed through the chapters, with each one providing a stepping stone to a more promising future in our education. Our research led us to the tools and methods that not only allow AI integration but also make it fun. We have revealed the wonders of AI, from tailor-made educational opportunities to streamlined office operations.

But don't forget about the AAA Method—it's what this whole journey is all about. I've given you the tools you need to confidently and successfully adapt to the rapidly evolving AI landscape: awareness, adaptability, and agility. As we've seen, AI is not some far-off, impossible-to-implement notion, but rather a practical tool that can improve your classroom and increase productivity.

One thing that is abundantly evident after reading this book is that AI is not a suitable substitute for human teachers but rather an invaluable ally. Being a strong force, it can make you an even better teacher and make the learning process more interesting and useful for your students. In other words, welcome AI with open arms because it will help you, not replace you.

Let's end on a positive note with pondering on a successful case. The amazing success account of Jill Watson at the Georgia Institute of Technology demonstrates the revolutionary impact of AI in education and serves as a prime example of the remarkable potential of AI in this field.

The increasing number of students in a master's level AI program was putting an undue strain on the available teaching assistants. The internet discussion board received roughly 10,000 new posts per semester, making it evident that conventional forms of support were unable to keep up. That's where Jill Watson, a virtual teaching assistant, stepped onto the scene.

The message board was inundated with the same kinds of queries, and Jill was made to handle that. She had stored up in her brain the answers to thousands upon thousands of questions from past semesters. The most impressive part of Jill's account is that her virtual assistant status went unnoticed by the majority of her students. An astonishing 97% of the time, Jill was able to correctly answer questions posed to her because she understood their context (Neelakantan, 2020).

Having said that, you may be asking if Jill's success has resulted in fewer jobs for human TAs. The answer is a resounding no. Jill wasn't meant to take over for human teachers; she was merely a helping hand. She was great at answering basic questions, but she lacked the ability to inspire her students or guide them through more complex assignments. She instead made room for the human TAs to concentrate on improving the classroom experience.

In the words of Jill's creator, Professor Ashok Goel, "Where humans cannot go, Jill will go. And what humans do not want to do, Jill can automate" (Neelakantan, 2020).

This statement perfectly captures the spirit of AI in education as a tool that gives teachers more control, improves students' experiences, and simplifies administrative tasks.

Jill's achievement exemplifies the vast potential that AI offers in the field of education. This serves as a gentle reminder that AI has not come to replace teachers, but rather to assist them by lightening their load so that they may focus more on developing the minds of the next generation.

Take Jill's experience to heart as we close this book. Accept the benefits that AI can bring to the classroom. Acknowledge that AI is a resource that can help you go further, improve the educational experience for your students, and shape a more promising future for learning.

Therefore, I encourage you to start your journey toward an education augmented by AI with the enthusiasm and self-assurance that come from what you have just learned. The great promise of AI can only be fully explored if people share their experiences of success, work together, and keep digging deeper. As an educator, you hold the keys to the future of learning, and with AI on your side, the opportunities are limitless.

Once again, your opinion is really valuable. Writing a review of this book or sharing it with a colleague to help spread its message is greatly appreciated.

References

Burns, E. (2022, July). *What is artificial intelligence (AI)?* TechTarget. https://www.techtarget.-
   com/searchenterpriseai/definition/AI-Artificial-Intelligence

Cisco. (2023, January 24). *92% of organizations think they need to do more to reassure
   customers about their data*. Newsroom Cisco. https://newsroom.cisco.com/c/r/news-
   room/en/us/a/y2023/m01/organizations-think-they-need-to-do-more-to-reassure-
   customers-about-how-their-data-is-used-in-ai-new-cisco-research.html

Copeland, B. J. (2019). *Artificial Intelligence—Alan Turing and the beginning of AI*. In
   Encyclopædia Britannica. https://www.britannica.com/technology/artificial-
   intelligence/Alan-Turing-and-the-beginning-of-AI

Department for Science, Innovation and Technology. (2023, April 19). *Cyber security
   breaches survey 2023*. GOV.UK. https://www.gov.uk/government/statistics/cyber-security-
   breaches-survey-2023/cyber-security-breaches-survey-2023

Future of Life Institute. (2023, March 22). *Pause giant AI experiments: An open letter*. Future
   of Life Institute. https://futureoflife.org/open-letter/pause-giant-ai-experiments/

George, A. (2023, May 31). *The importance of artificial intelligence in education for all
   students*. Language Magazine. https://www.languagemagazine.com/2023/05/31/the-
   importance-of-artificial-intelligence-in-education-for-all-students/

Gopalasamy, P. (2022, October 28). *Navigating the CPRA's "do not sell or share"
   requirement*. OneTrust. https://www.onetrust.com/blog/navigating-the-cpras-do-not-sell-
   or-share-requirement/

Hardison, H. (2022, April 19). *How teachers spend their time: A breakdown*. Education Week.
   https://www.edweek.org/teaching-learning/how-teachers-spend-their-time-a-
   breakdown/2022/04

Hardman, D. P. (2023, March 23). *A brief history of AI in education*. Dr Philippa Hardman
   Substack. https://drphilippahardman.substack.com/p/a-brief-history-of-ai-in-education

Henebery, B. (2023, March 28). *Reducing admin tasks boosts teacher morale, study finds*.
   The Educator Online. https://www.theeducatoronline.com/k12/news/reducing-admin-
   tasks-boosts-teacher-morale-study-finds/282229

Inc, G. M. I. (2021, June 23). *AI in education market revenue to cross $20B by 2027; Global
   Market Insights, Inc*. PR Newswire. https://www.prnewswire.com/news-releases/ai-in-
   education-market-revenue-to-cross-20b-by-2027-global-market-insights-inc-
   301318889.html

Intersoft Consulting. (n.d.). *Art. 22 GDPR – Automated individual decision-making, including
   profiling*. General Data Protection Regulation (GDPR). https://gdpr-info.eu/art-22-gdpr/

Klein, A. (2023, May 15). *Students and parents are bullish on AI's potential for education.*

References

Education Week. https://www.edweek.org/technology/students-and-parents-are-bullish-on-ais-potential-for-education/2023/05

Malekos, N. (2023, April 19). *The rise of artificial intelligence in education: will A.I. disrupt eLearning?* Learn Worlds. https://www.learnworlds.com/artificial-intelligence-in-education/

Munson, L. (2023, May 6). *AI quotes about the artificial intelligence world*. Everyday Power. https://everydaypower.com/ai-quotes/

MurfResources. (2023, July 25). *Choosing the best: 2023's top 10 speech to text Applications*. Murf.ai. https://murf.ai/resources/top-speech-to-text-softwares/#:~:text=Nuance%20Dragon

Neelakantan, S. (2020, January 2). *Successful AI examples in higher education that can inspire our future*. Technology Solutions That Drive Education. https://edtechmagazine.com/higher/article/2020/01/successful-ai-examples-higher-education-can-inspire-our-future

OpenAI. (2023, August 31). *Teaching with AI*. OpenAI. https://openai.com/blog/teaching-with-ai

Ortiz, S. (2023, April 18). *What Is chatGPT and why does It matter? Here's everything you need to know*. ZDNET. https://www.zdnet.com/article/what-is-chatgpt-and-why-does-it-matter-heres-everything-you-need-to-know/

State of California Department of Justice. (2023, May 10). *California consumer privacy act (CCPA)*. State of California - Department of Justice - Office of the Attorney General. https://oag.ca.gov/privacy/ccpa

The White House. (2022). *Blueprint for an AI bill of rights*. The White House. https://www.whitehouse.gov/ostp/ai-bill-of-rights/

Thompson, J. (2021, June 1). *58% of secondary schools faced cyber attacks last year*. NWCRC. https://www.nwcrc.co.uk/post/58-of-secondary-schools-faced-cyber-attacks-last-year-government-figures-show

University of Washington. (n.d.). *Engaging students*. Teaching@UW. https://teaching.washington.edu/engaging-students/

Printed in Great Britain
by Amazon

36249764R00068